JOSHU.   'AN

MW00861448

Social Media as Evidence

CASES, PRACTICE POINTERS, AND TECHNIQUES

ABA **LawPracticeManagementSection**
MARKETING • MANAGEMENT • TECHNOLOGY • FINANCE

Commitment to Quality: The Law Practice Management Section is committed to quality in our publications. Our authors are experienced practitioners in their fields. Prior to publication, the contents of all our books are rigorously reviewed by experts to ensure the highest quality product and presentation. Because we are committed to serving our readers' needs, we welcome your feedback on how we can improve future editions of this book.

Cover design by RIPE Creative, Inc.

Printed in the United States of America.

16 15 14 13 5 4 3 2 1

Library of Congress Cataloging-in-Publication Data

Briones, Joshua.
    Social media as evidence : cases, practice pointers, and techniques / Joshua Briones and Ana Tagvoryan.
      pages cm
      Includes index.
      ISBN 978-1-61438-629-2
      1. Electronic evidence--United States. 2. Social media--Law and legislation--United States. I. Tagvoryan, Ana. II. American Bar Association. Section of Law Practice Management. III. Title.
      KF8947.5.B75 2013
      347.73'6--dc23
                                                                    2013003084

Discounts are available for books ordered in bulk. Special consideration is given to state bars, CLE programs, and other bar-related organizations. Inquire at Book Publishing, American Bar Association, 321 North Clark Street, Chicago, Illinois 60654-7598.

www.ShopABA.org

About the Authors

 Joshua Briones is a partner in his firm's Litigation group and co-chair of the firm's Social Media practice group. He regularly counsels clients on Internet and social media legal issues, as well as issues relating to records retention, litigation holds, and the preservation and use of social media and other electronic data. Since 2011, Mr. Briones has been named a Southern California Rising Star.

 Ana Tagvoryan is in her firm's Litigation Group and a member of her firm's Social Media practice group. She frequently gives seminars on the topic and is the co-author of numerous articles and publications about social media, privacy, and related class actions. Her clients also rely on her expertise as an effective crisis manager and litigation counselor.

Preface

Times have changed. The world's population now spends more than 110 billion minutes on social networks and blog sites each month. The way in which we prepare for and try cases must take into account the types of communication media now in use. Simply put, trials involve witnesses, and it is likely that the modern witness has an electronic trail or history that may be relevant and/or persuasive when making your case or trying to break down your opposition.

This book is for, and dedicated to, civil litigators who, while running a busy law practice, frequently face the pressures of trying to catch up with the latest changes in the fields in which they practice. Then, of course, they are supposed to know all the ground rules governing the litigation process … rules that are constantly being rewritten, refined, and generally tinkered with by legislatures and our courts.

This book is therefore designed to offer reliable help with the rules and authorities related to the use of social media data as evidence in a civil action:

- We cover each stage of pretrial proceedings, setting forth the applicable rules as clearly and simply as possible, with key practice pointers to illustrate the rules' application.

- Our aim is to keep this book up to date by rewriting it frequently to eliminate obsolete material and to include new trends as they develop.

- We do not cover the logistics of finding and searching through social media profiles. For more information on the practical aspects of social media use, see Carole Levitt and Mark Rosch, *Find Info Like a Pro,* v. 1 (ABA, 2010) and Carole Levitt and Mark Rosch, *The Cyber-sleuth's Guide to the Internet,* 12th ed. (IFL Press, 2012).

Obviously, no book can substitute for independent research and analysis in a particular case. But we think we have provided the basic information needed to handle problems commonly encountered when social media data is involved in civil litigation, as well as some pointers that will enable you to practice more confidently and successfully!

Joshua Briones   Ana Tagvoryan

Acknowledgments

Lindsey Dodge, Crystal Lopez, Stephanie Smith, and Esteban Morales

This book would not have come into being without the support and hard work of Lindsey Dodge, Crystal Lopez, Stephanie Smith, and Esteban Morales.

Jeffrey Brockway

The authors wish to thank Jeffrey Brockway for his graphical contributions to this book.

Carole Levitt and Denise Constantine

We are grateful to fellow ABA author Carole Levitt and the Manager of Book Publishing at the American Bar Association, Denise Constantine, for shepherding the book through the initial approval stages, providing feedback on the initial drafts, and for their tireless work to get the book to press.

Contents

See of the first pages of each chapter for a detailed list of contents.

Chapter Contents

Chapter 1: Introduction to Social Media

Chapter 1

Introduction to Social Media

1. Why Lawyers Need to Understand Social Media

[1:1] **Social Media Is an Evidentiary Gold Mine:**
Social media has become an evidentiary gold mine for impeaching witnesses and undermining a party's litigation position. The proverbial "smoking gun" document of the pre-Internet era, which had given way to the smoking gun e-mail, has now given way to the smoking gun social media post. As in the early days of e-mail, postings on social media sites tend to be colloquial, casual, and lacking many of the usual constraints found in more formal communications. There is also a misperception that information on social media sites is private or limited to "friends" of the poster. In reality, much of the information on social media sites is not private, and it can often be accessed or seen by complete strangers.

3

[1:2] **Explosive Growth:** Eighty percent of Americans who are online now regularly use some form of social media. By the end of 2012, the statistics were staggering: 200 million blogs worldwide, 901 million monthly active users on Facebook, more than 260 million users on Myspace, 160 million users on LinkedIn, 340 million tweets every 24 hours, and 4 billion YouTube views each day [*see* pewinternet.org]. These numbers reflect the explosive growth social media has experienced over the past five years. Many users of these popular sites catalogue their lives with surprising honesty and detail, without regard for the possible legal ramifications of their posts. (Fig. 1.1)

Figure 1.1   Social Networking Growth Chart

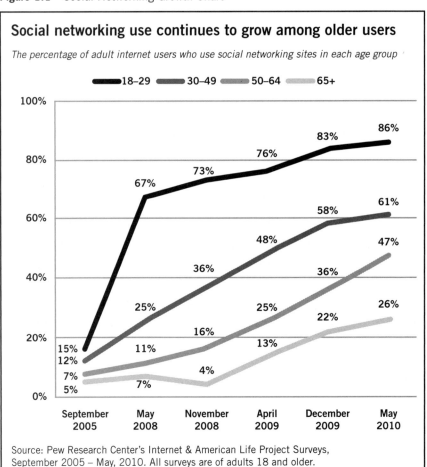

Social networking use continues to grow among older users

The percentage of adult internet users who use social networking sites in each age group

18–29   30–49   50–64   65+

Source: Pew Research Center's Internet & American Life Project Surveys, September 2005 – May, 2010. All surveys are of adults 18 and older.

E-mail is less relevant by the day. In 2012, most people between the ages 12 and 54 used e-mail less frequently than the year before; Boston College even stopped issuing e-mail accounts to incoming freshmen. [http://tinyurl.com/997ezhr]

[1:3] Social Media Affects Data Retention / Destruction Policies: In light of this explosive growth and its pervasive nature, social media clearly expands the universe of potentially discoverable materials and affects data retention/destruction policies. Just as requests for e-mails were the discovery rage of the last decade, requests for information on social media platforms will soon become standard. These new technologies are dramatically changing the discovery landscape. In a February 17, 2011, press release the consulting firm Gartner, Inc., stated that by 2013 nearly half of all U.S. companies will be asked to produce social media data in discovery. [Gartner, Inc. press release published at www.efytimes.com/e1/58912/fullnews.htm (last visited May 27, 2012).]

[1:4] Litigation Will Soon Regularly Involve Social Media Data as Evidence: There is therefore little question that litigation will regularly involve social media data as evidence. Moreover, as clients begin to adopt these new social media technologies, they will expect the lawyers who advise them to understand how these new communication platforms operate and what new legal risks are created. For this reason, it is important for litigators to understand what social media is and how to talk about it. This chapter covers various preliminary considerations, key words and definitions, and concepts regarding social media.

2. What Is Social Media and Where Does the Data Reside?

[1:5] **Social Media Defined:** Social media sites are web-based services that allow individuals to construct a public or semi-public profile within a bounded system, articulate a list of other users with whom they share a connection, and view and share their list of connections and those made by others within the system. For our purposes, this definition empha-sizes two primary activities on such sites: *First,* unlike employer- or corporate-specific e-mail, for example, the data that is created on social media sites is web based and is there-fore often stored off-site by the social media service provider. *Second,* users create a unique online identity, establish rela-tionships with other users, and join various communities of users who share connections.

To create a common frame of reference, we will first briefly describe a few of the most popular social media sites with a focus on how users generate data. We will then discuss where that data is generally stored and how it may be accessed.

[1:5:1] **Brief Description of Popular Social Media Sites:**

[1:5:1:1] **Facebook:** Facebook currently is the most popular social-networking website. In general, Facebook allows users—private individuals or corporate entities—to create online profiles that display information about themselves and/or their entities and share that information with others, such as:

[1:5:1:1:1] **Text Updates:** Facebook users can share text with multiple people through a "status update" or through infor-mation placed on the user's profile. Users can also share text with another user individually through a direct message to the user or a wall post to another user's profile, or users can have a direct conversation with another user through Facebook's chat feature.

[1:5:1:1:2] **Photographs and Videos:** Facebook users may share pictures and videos and may specifically identify who can view each one. When posting photographs to Facebook, users may identify themselves or other site members by name, a process known as "tagging." A photo tag creates a link to that user's profile and identifies the person and his or her specific location in the photo. Anyone with access to a given user's photos can view photos in which that user is tagged, including group photos of that user and others identified by name. Users may also "comment" on photos.

[1:5:1:1:3] **Sharing Links and "Liking":** A Facebook user may also communicate via the "like" button, which allows him or her to "like" other users' communications or photographs and those of his or her own. Users can also share links, videos, photographs and/or text with other users.

PRACTICE POINTER

By way of example, the average Facebook profile contains a wealth of potentially discoverable information. Profiles can include a person's hometown, date of birth, address, occupation, ethnicity, height, relationship status, income, education, associations, "likes," and a limitless array of comments, messages, photographs, and videos that reside in the "public" domain and are not likely to be filtered by opposing counsel.

> **PRACTICE POINTER**
>
> All of this means there is a potential treasure trove of evidence in various forms on a social media site like Facebook, e.g., photographs, videos, and other activity, which, depending on the type of case, could be relevant to key issues in the action.

[1:5:1:2] **Twitter:** Twitter allows users to share messages of 140 characters or fewer (referred to as a tweet). Messages may be shared with specified people or the public at large. Users can send messages and view others' messages through the Internet via a computer or mobile device. Twitter users also may share pictures with other users. Users who choose to have private Twitter accounts display their tweets only to specifically authorized persons. Users who have public accounts display their tweets to the public. It is also possible to "follow" a Twitter user and thereby gather background information and intelligence about that user.

> **PRACTICE POINTER**
>
> Twitter could be fruitful in providing access to the individuals and entities that a user is following, and thereby allow others to deduce intelligence about the user. For example, if the user is following President Barack Obama, one might deduce that the user is Democrat and/or liberal. If the user is a potential juror, this intelligence might help inform whether a conservative Republican is a good fit for the particular trial.

[1:5:1:3] **Myspace (previously MySpace):** Similar to Facebook, Myspace allows a user to interact with other Myspace users. For example, a user can share pictures and videos with a friends list. Myspace also enables a user to post on a "bulletin board" that is visible to his or her Myspace friends. Bulletins can be useful for contacting an entire friends list instead of messaging users individually. Although bulletins are deleted after ten days, they have become the primary attack point for phishing, which is typically an attempt to scam users to surrender private information that will be used for identity theft.

In early 2006, Myspace introduced MySpace IM, an instant messenger. A user logs in using the e-mail associated with his or her Myspace account. Unlike other parts of Myspace, MySpace IM is stand-alone software for Microsoft Windows. Users who use this messenger get instant notification of new Myspace messages, friend requests, and comments. In early 2007, Myspace introduced MySpace TV, a service similar to the YouTube video-sharing website. Myspace also has a status update feature, which allows a user with a Twitter account to update the Myspace status with each tweet (Facebook also has a similar feature). Myspace profiles contain two standard "blurbs": About Me and Who I'd Like to Meet sections. Profiles also contain sections for Interests and Details. Status and Zodiac Sign fields always display in the Details section.

PRACTICE POINTER

Social media sites like Myspace have been the source of discoveries previously thought unimaginable based on their private nature. For example, photographs of people performing sexually suggestive acts while dressed up like Santa Claus and violently vomiting after overindulging on alcoholic beverages have emerged on Myspace [see *Mackelprang v. Fidelity Nat'l Title Agency of Nev., Inc.*, No. 2:06-CV-0078-JCM-GWF, 2007 WL 119149 (D. Nev. Jan. 9, 2007), http://tinyurl.com/9bopo8w discussed below at [2:12]].

[1:5:1:4] **LinkedIn:** LinkedIn allows registered users to maintain a list of people with whom they have some level of relationship, called Connections. Users can view information about their Connections and contact them through the site. Users can invite anyone (whether a site user or not) to become a connection. This list of connections can then be used in a number of ways: A contact network is built up consisting of direct connections, the connections of each of their connections (termed second-degree connections), and also the connections of second-degree connections (termed third-degree connections). This network can be used to gain an introduction to someone a person wishes to know through a mutual contact. Users can upload their resume or design their own profile to showcase work, educational background, and community experiences. Users can post their own photos and view photos of others to aid in identification. Users can save (i.e., bookmark) jobs for which they would like to apply.

PRACTICE POINTER

Users often post full resumes with detailed histories of their past employment. LinkedIn is therefore an excellent resource that can be used to impeach a witness during a deposition or at trial if he or she contradicts information posted on the site.

[1:5:1:5] **YouTube:** YouTube is a video-sharing website on which users can upload, view, and share videos. The company uses Adobe Flash Video and HTML5 technology to display a wide variety of user-generated video content, including movie clips, TV clips, and music videos, as well as amateur content such as video blogging and short original videos. Most of the content on YouTube has been uploaded by individuals, although as part of the YouTube partnership program, media corporations including CBS, the BBC, VEVO, Hulu, and other organizations offer some of their material via the site. Unregistered users can watch videos, while registered users can upload an unlimited number of videos. Videos considered to contain potentially offensive content are available only to registered users at least 18 years old. In November 2006, YouTube, LLC was bought by Google for $1.65 billion, and now operates as a subsidiary of Google.

> **PRACTICE POINTER**
>
> Anyone can post a video on YouTube. As a result, attorneys would do well to search the site for potential evidence involving the parties or witnesses, especially in cases in which physical activity is at issue.

[1:5:2] Where Does the Data Reside and How Is It Accessed?

[1:5:2:1] Access to Data on Social Media Sites and Blogs: On social media sites like Facebook or LinkedIn, a user's privacy settings dictate who can access to information contained on that user's profile. For example, a person must be a "friend" of a Facebook user to access his or her Private page if the user has restricted his or her profile to "friends only." Other settings expand the access to "friends of friends" or even "everyone," and one setting restricts the profile to "only me." A user's private comments on Facebook can be copied and pasted elsewhere, and thus may become generally accessible on the Internet beyond what the profile owner ever intended. Blog posts are generally readily accessible by any Internet user. Public tweets and public profiles can be accessed by any third party online.

[1:5:2:2] Storage of Social Media: Storage of social media information is complicated. Tweets are stored on Twitter's servers unless deleted by the sender, but they also may be stored on the servers of mobile phone providers or other application providers. Facebook information, and that of other social media sites such as Myspace and LinkedIn, is stored on Facebook's servers. Users can download their Facebook and Twitter accounts to their own computers, so that a copy of social media data can also be stored locally.

Chapter Contents

Chapter 2: Retrieval and Retention of Social Media Data

Chapter 2

Retrieval and Retention of Social Media Data

1. Introduction

[2:1] **Potentially Relevant Social Media Data May Need to Be Preserved for Litigation:** Just like other forms of electronically stored information, social media materials may need to be preserved for potential disclosure or discovery *if those materials contain relevant information.*

[2:2] **Preserving Social Media Data Presents Unique Challenges:** The preservation of social media data, however, may present unique challenges. Websites like Facebook and Twitter are dynamic; users constantly add and delete posts. To overcome these authentication and preservation challenges, social media data must be properly collected, preserved, searched, and produced in a manner consistent with best practices. When social media is collected with a proper chain of custody and all associated metadata is preserved, authenticity is much easier to establish.

PRACTICE POINTER

Compared with preserving the Word files employees create, accurately preserving social media can be extremely complicated. It requires knowing how application programming interfaces (APIs) work. Software programs communicate with each other through APIs. When archiving social media, it is important to consider whether the solution is actually pulling data from an API or simply taking a "screen shot" of what can be viewed in a browser. A screen shot won't include metadata or other information that can't be "seen," but which may be critically important in a lawsuit and/or to authenticate the data.

---

2. Duty to Preserve Social Media as "Electronically Stored Information"

[2:3] *Zubulake v. UBS Warburg LLC*—**Duty to Preserve Extends to All Electronically Stored Information:** The leading case in this area is *Zubulake v. UBS Warburg LLC*. In a series of opinions issued in *Zubulake*, Judge Shira A. Scheindlin of the Southern District of New York provided some guidance on whether a corporate party has a duty to preserve social media data. While the opinions and underlying facts do not directly involve social media, the principles espoused are instructive. In *Zubulake*, Judge Scheindlin held that a party's duty to preserve evidence extends to all electronically stored information that a party knows, or reasonably should know, is relevant to the subject matter of the litigation. [*Zubulake v. UBS Warburg LLC*, 220 F.R.D. 212, 217 (S.D.N.Y. 2003), http://tinyurl.

com/8k3w8yt] This expansive definition necessarily includes social media data.

[2:4] **Rule 34(a)(1) "E-Discovery Amendments" Suggest Duty to Preserve Social Media Data:** In December of 2006, the Advisory Committee on the Federal Rules of Civil Procedure's "E-discovery Amendments" went into effect, "confirm[ing] that discovery of electronically stored information stands on equal footing with discovery of paper documents." [Fed. R. Civ. P. 34 Committee Notes on Rules – 2006 Amendment.] Under its new guise, Rule 34(a)(1) allows parties to request the production, inspection, copying, testing, or sampling of electronically stored information that is within the responding party's possession, custody, or control. [Fed. R. Civ. P. 34(a).] The Committee Notes explain that Rule 34(a)(1) "is expansive and includes any type of information that is stored electronically." [Fed. R. Civ. Proc. 34 Committee Notes on Rules – 2006 Amendment.]

[2:4:1] **Rule 34(a)(1)'s Language Poses Unique Problems That Have Yet to Be Resolved by the Courts in the Context of Social Media:** For instance, in the event that a company's employee corresponds over Facebook or Myspace regarding information relevant to a suit, is that company in "possession, custody, or control" of the pertinent information? Although this area of the law is in its infancy, the following case provides practical guidelines based on recent decisions indicating 1) data created on a company's social media page is likely information in its possession, custody, or control,- and 2) that prudent parties should inform employees of the need to preserve potentially relevant information created using personal social media accounts.

[2:4:2] **Scope of Rule 34(a) Includes Social Media:** In *Columbia Pictures*, the United States District Court for the Central District of California addressed whether data *temporarily stored* in a computer's random access memory, or RAM, qualifies as electronically stored information for purposes of Rule 34. The court held that it did. In reaching its holding, the District Court was guided by technological change that "counsel[s] against a limiting or precise definition of electronically stored information" and the Advisory Committee's notes that accompany Rule 34. [*Columbia Pictures, Inc. v. Bunnell, et al.*, 245 F.R.D. 443, 447 (C.D. Cal. 2007).] Noting that electronic messages qualify as electronically stored information, the District Court pointed to "Rule 34(a)'s scope [which] was intended to be as broad as possible," and held that ephemeral, or temporarily stored data also qualifies as electronically stored information. [*Id.* at 446.]

PRACTICE POINTER

In the context of Rule 34's broad Committee Notes, and decisions such as *Columbia Pictures,* which interpreted Rule 34(a)(1) to capture *any* information stored electronically, it is unlikely that a court would hold that information on a social media website should not be considered electronically stored information. Consequently, the same principles that require parties to preserve electronically stored information apply to data and activity on social media websites.

[2:5] **IT Policy Could Affect Determination on Whether Duty to Preserve Extends to Social Media:** If, for example, a company's IT policy states that the business owns everything created, stored, sent, or received on company equipment, then a court might find that the company arguably owns— and therefore controls—any social media created by an employee at work or on a company computer. [*Zubulake*, 220 F.R.D. at 218.] One of the key issues addressed by Judge Scheindlin in *Zubulake v. UBS Warburg LLC* is whether discovery obligations reach the electronically stored information of "key players" in a dispute. A "key player" in a dispute is anyone at the company who is likely to have relevant information. Judge Scheindlin held that discovery obligations do indeed extend to the electronically stored information of key players.

PRACTICE POINTER

The laws of employee privacy and social media are far from settled, however, and a finding of "control" might not be made so easily. Nevertheless, a company's IT policy and the manner in which its "key players" communicate with employees are important to the issue of control. If a key player has been communicating about the subject matter of the dispute, courts may take a dim view of purposeful attempts to circumvent discovery obligations by conducting those communications through networks that are not directly within the physical control of the party to the litigation, such as is the case with nearly all social media sites. Companies should therefore update their document retention policy to include social media activity. The procedures that the company is following for e-mails in terms of storage and retention periods may be a good starting point. By having established processes and following them, adversaries in litigation will have a hard time arguing that the company has destroyed relevant, and possibly damaging, information. The standard for preservation is "reasonableness and proportionality," so modeling it after the procedure for retention of company e-mails makes sense and is internally consistent.

[2:6] **Industry Regulations Suggest that Social Media Data Should Be Retained and Preserved:** The revisions to the document retention policy should also take into consideration any industry regulations, such as state laws governing real estate brokers, and SEC and FINRA record-keeping rules for the financial services industry.

[2:6:1] **FINRA:** For example, FINRA issued guidance in January 2010 for blogs and social networking sites and set forth the record keeping responsibilities in the financial broker-dealer business. "Every firm that intends to communicate, or permit its associated persons to communicate, through social media sites must first ensure that it can retain records of those communications as required by Rules 17a-3 and 17a-4 under the Securities Exchange Act of 1934 and NASD Rule 3110."

[2:6:2] **SEC Alert:** In January 2012, the SEC issued an alert regarding the use of social media by investment advisers. The alert emphasized that investment firms "that communicate through social media must retain records of those communications if they contain information that satisfies an investment adviser's recordkeeping obligations under the Advisers Act." The alert also set out a non-exhaustive list of factors relating to the recordkeeping and production requirements of required records generated by social media communications, including access and retrieval. (SEC Alert published at http://tinyurl. com/9rnud3s (last accessed September 27, 2012).)

[2:7] **Case Law Suggests Duty to Preserve Social Media Data in Certain Circumstances:** As of yet, no court appears to have explicitly stated that information on social media sites qualifies as "electronically stored information." Nonetheless, several decisions suggest that social media qualifies.

[2:7:1] **Social Media Data Is Discoverable from a Party:** In *Mackelprang v. Fidelity Nat'l Title Agency of Nev., Inc.,* No. 2:06-CV-0078-JCM-GWF, 2007 WL 119149 (D. Nev. Jan. 9, 2007), http://tinyurl.com/9bopo8w, the court held that the proper method for obtaining relevant information is to serve upon the party properly limited requests for discovery of relevant communications. In *Mackelprang,* following the plaintiff's filing of a suit for, among other things, sexual harassment, the defendant, Fidelity, issued a subpoena directly to Myspace. com seeking e-mail communications made using two Myspace.com accounts allegedly set up by the plaintiff. [*Id.* at

*1-*2.] In response, however, Myspace.com merely produced the dates on which the accounts were created and the number of times the user had logged into the account during the relevant time period. Myspace.com, however, refused to produce private e-mail messages on either account. Fidelity filed a Motion to Compel. [*Id.* at *2.] Finding that Fidelity had no information regarding the identities of the persons with whom Plaintiff had exchanged private e-mail messages or the subject matter of the e-mail messages, the court denied Fidelity's Motion. [*Id.* at *2 and *9.] The court noted, however, that the "proper method for obtaining such information . . . is to *serve upon Plaintiff* properly limited requests for production of relevant e-mail communications." [*Id.* at *8 (emphasis added).]

[2:7:2] **Website Is Under Company's "Control" (And Therefore Social Media Data Should be Preserved) Where Company Can Modify Content:** In at least two decisions, *Katiroll Co., Inc. v. Kati Roll and Platters, Inc.*, and *Arteria Property Pty Ltd. V. Universal Funding V.T.O.*, courts have held that when a company has "ultimate" authority over its website, the website is within the company's control.

[2:7:2:1] **"Ultimate" Authority Over Website Means Control:** In a trademark dispute between restaurants, the plaintiff brought a sanctions motion claiming spoliation of the defendant's Facebook profile. [*Katiroll Co. v. Kati Roll & Platters, Inc.*, 2011 U.S. Dist. LEXIS 85212, 1-2 (D.N.J. Aug. 3, 2011).] The defendant argued that sanctions were not warranted because its Facebook profile was a public website, which Plaintiff could have preserved itself. In reaching its holding, the *Katiroll* court noted that prior courts had held that public websites are still within the control of those who own the websites. The *Katiroll* court stated, "Given that Defendants have a discovery obligation to produce them and that only Defendants knew when the website would be changed, it is more appropriate for

Defendants to have that burden." The court therefore held that because the company had "*ultimate*" authority over its website, the website was within the defendant's control.

[2:7:2:2] **Whether Maintained by a Third Party Is Irrelevant:** The *Katiroll* court made reference to *Arteria Property Pty Ltd. v. Universal Funding V.T.O., Inc.*, which involved a spoliation dispute stemming from, among other things, the destruction of a company website. [*Arteria Prop. Pty Ltd. v. Universal Funding V.T.O., Inc.*, No. 05-4896 (PGS), 2008 WL 4513696 (D.N.J. Oct. 1, 2008), http://tinyurl.com/9vyc3zr] As in *Katiroll*, the *Arteria Property* court held that the defendants' website was under the defendants' "control" for purposes of a spoliation analysis. [*Id.* at *5.] The *Arteria Property,* court added that whether the website was maintained by a third party, or whether it was maintained on a third party server, was "irrelevant." [*Id.*] Because the defendants or company "had the *ultimate* authority, and thus control, to add, delete, or modify the website's content," the website was deemed within the defendants' control. [*Id.*]

[2:7:3] **Website Is Under Party's "Control" (And Therefore Social Media Data Should Be Preserved) Where Party Can Allow Access to Information on Website:** *Netbula, LLC v. Chordiant Software, Inc.*, indicates that, as in *Katiroll* and *Arteria*, so long as a party can modify or allow access to information on a website, the company will be found to be in "control" for purposes of Rule 34(a)(1). Defendants in *Netbula* filed a motion to compel Plaintiff to allow access to Plaintiff's past web pages that had been archived by the Internet Archive, a non-party that provided access to archived websites via an internet website called the "Wayback Machine." [*Netbula, LLC v. Chordiant Software, Inc.*, No. C08-00019 JW (HRL), 2009 WL 3352588, at *1 (N.D. Cal. Oct. 15, 2009), http://tinyurl.com/9t28sz7] Plaintiff had prevented the public from accessing the Wayback

Machine's archives of Plaintiff's website by placing a file designed for this purpose on Plaintiff's website. Plaintiff attempted to avoid having Defendants' motion granted by arguing that for purposes of Rule 34(a)(1), they lacked "control" over the information sought. The court disagreed, holding that Plaintiff controlled information on the website because it controlled access to the archived pages. [*Id.*]

Although courts have yet to address whether data on a corporate party's social media page falls within the "control" of the party, the analyses in *Katiroll*, *Arteria*, and *Netbula* indicate that faced with this question, a court would answer affirmatively as companies, and by extension their authorized employees, have the authority to add, delete, and control access to information on their social media pages. Consequently, companies and those employees involved must be prepared to preserve relevant information on the company's social media web pages once the duty to preserve is triggered.

[2:7:4] **Data Created by an Employee on a Non-Company Social Media Page or Site:** Whether a court would find that information created by employees on a non-company social media page or site is "electronically stored information" within a corporate party's "possession, custody, or control" is less clear. Corporate parties may have a duty to preserve relevant information where employees use social media for business purposes. Others speculate that companies may be held to "control" social media information where they inform their employees that information created using the employer's computer and communications systems belongs to the company. This same reasoning would likely apply if the employee was updating or using the company's social media site from a personal or home computer.

[2:7:5] **Companies May Be Held to "Control" Employees' Personal Social Media Data:** *In re Triton Energy Ltd. Sec. Litig.*

involved information stored on former outside directors' home computers and hinged on whether potentially relevant information existed on those computers. This case suggests that courts may hold employers responsible for preserving social media information created using their employees' personal social media accounts. [*In re Triton Energy Ltd. Sec. Litig.*, No. 5:98CV256, 2002 WL 32114464 (E.D. Tex. Mar. 7, 2002), http:// tinyurl.com/9xpgpj7] Plaintiffs in *In re Triton* filed a motion for a log of withheld documents, for certification of preservation and retention of documents, and for the production of the defendant's computer storage systems after deposition testimony raised concerns regarding the destruction of evidence. [*Id.* at *1.] The court granted Plaintiffs' motion, and appointed a forensic computer specialist to retrieve information from the defendant's computer storage systems as well as the home computers of former officers and directors. [*Id.* at *6.] "[I]t would have been prudent and within the spirit of the law for Triton to instruct its officers and directors to preserve and produce any documents in their possession, custody, or control," concluded the court. [*Id.*] While the *In re Triton* case expressly involved the home computers of former outside directors, the ruling did not turn so much on whether the person involved was an outside director as it did on whether he or she had potentially relevant information on their home computers. Accordingly, a company may be held to "control" *any* employees' personal social media data if that employee is held to have control of or access to evidence that is relevant to the action.

> **PRACTICE POINTER**
>
> *Triton* provides lessons for both plaintiff and defense attorneys.
>
> **Plaintiffs:** From a plaintiff's perspective, the lesson of *Triton* is to consider *all* the areas/people where potentially relevant information may exist and to propound well-crafted and specific discovery requests that seek this information.
>
> **Defendants:** On the defense side, employers should prepare to preserve relevant data—if they have control of or access to it—on employee personal social media accounts. Though courts have not ruled on whether information created by employees using their personal social media accounts is discoverable and subject to a corporate party's preservation duty, decisions like *In re Triton* and *U&I Corp.* indicate that commentators may be correct, and that employers have a duty to preserve relevant information on their employees' personal social media pages. Employers should thus consider including language in their litigation holds designed to preserve potentially relevant social media information created by the employer *and employees* using personal social media accounts.

[2:7:6] **Access to Employees' Social Media Profiles Could Also Affect Determination on Whether a Company Exercises Control:** Although less likely, a business that can gain access to an employee's social media profiles, by, for example, compelling the employee to divulge log-in information, might also have sufficient ability to access those records to be in "control" of them.

> **PRACTICE POINTER**
>
> In light of the above, companies should update their document retention policy to include social media activity. The procedures that the company is following for e-mails in terms of storage and retention periods may be a good starting point. By having established processes and following them, adversaries in litigation will have a hard time arguing that the company has destroyed relevant, and possibly damaging, information. The standard for preservation is "reasonableness and proportionality," so modeling it after the procedure for retention of company e-mails makes sense and is internally consistent.

3. Spoliation of Social Media Data

[2:8] **Failure to Preserve Potentially Relevant Evidence Has Resulted in Big Sanctions:** A recent study found that courts are increasingly imposing large sanctions against attorneys and their clients for failing to comply with e-discovery rules. In a study of 401 cases in which sanctions were sought before 2010, sanctions were awarded in more than half. [http://tinyurl.com/6h7lyby] Some of the sanctions were especially severe, including dismissal of cases, adverse jury instructions, and large monetary sanctions. Sanctions of $5 million were ordered in five cases, and $1 million or more in four others. Defendants were sanctioned for e-discovery violations nearly three times more often than Plaintiffs, and the number one reason for imposing sanctions was failure to preserve electronic evidence.

[2:9] **Sanctions for Failing to Preserve Documents on Employees' Personal Home Computers:** In the context of a motion to compel and motion for sanctions, in *U&I Corp. v. Advanced Medical Design*, the District Court for the Middle District of

Florida sanctioned a defendant's failure to document its efforts to locate and produce e-mails contained in home personal computers of the defendant's employees. [*U&I Corp. v. Advanced Med. Design, Inc.*, 251 F.R.D. 667, 675 (M.D. Fla. 2008).] Before issuing sanctions, the court noted that the defendant "fail[ed] to submit an affidavit from a knowledgeable individual verifying the scope of the search, the efforts taken to locate documents, the inability to identify and produce such documents and the date when these documents were deleted or removed from **the personal computers**." [*Id.* (emphasis added).] The court's emphasis on the defendant's failure to produce e-mails from home personal computers and to document its efforts to locate these e-mails indicates that the defendant failed to satisfy its duty to preserve documents on home personal computers of its employees. The reasoning in this case suggests the very same principles could be applied to social media data on home personal computers of its employees.

[2:10] **Sanctions for Instructing Client to "Clean-Up" Facebook Account:** At least one court has held that spoliation of social media evidence is just like the spoliation of any other evidence [see hytechlawyer.com/wp-content/uploads/2012/01/facebook-spoiliation.pdf]. A state court in Virginia ordered a prominent Virginia trial attorney, Matthew Murray, to pay over $522,000 in sanctions for instructing his client to "clean up" his Facebook page. [*Id.*] The court found that Murray told his client to remove several photos from his Facebook account on fears that they would prejudice his wrongful death case brought after his spouses' fatal automobile accident. Murray instructed his client through his assistant to 'clean up' his Facebook account: "We do not want blow ups of other pics at trial," the assistant's e-mail to Lester said, "so please, please clean up your Facebook and MySpace!" The court also found that Murray instructed the client to deactivate his Facebook account so that on the day that discovery responses were submitted the attorney's response could be, and was, that the client did not have a Facebook account.

4. Litigation Holds

[2:11] **Litigation Hold Must Include Social Media Data to Avoid Sanctions:** In light of this recent rise of sanctions in connection with e-discovery violations and explosive growth in the use of social media, the parties who fail to consider preserving potentially relevant social media data risk exposure to spoliation sanctions ranging from adverse inference jury instructions to extreme sanctions, such as dismissals of claims. Parties can avoid these pitfalls by creating and implementing an effective preservation strategy that takes social media data into account.

[2:11:1] **Litigation Hold Should Also Include Nonemployee Directors:** The District Court in *In re Triton*, discussed above, admonished a party for failing to advise nonemployee outside directors, who were not named as parties to the suit, to preserve potentially relevant information. [*In re Triton Energy*, 2002 WL 32114464 at *3-4.] "The Court [was] of the opinion that it would have been prudent and within the spirit of the law for Triton to instruct" the nonemployee outside directors to preserve such information. [*Id.* at *6.]

[2:11:2] **Duty to Instruct Third Party E-mail, File Server, and Electronic-Data-Related Disaster Recovery Provider to Preserve Data:** In *Keir v. UnumProvident Corp.*, the United States District Court for the Southern District of New York suggested that Defendant UnumProvident Corp. should have effectively communicated to IBM the need to preserve documents. IBM was a nonparty that provided e-mail, file server, and electronic-data-related disaster recovery services to the defendant, in order to satisfy its preservation duty. [*Keir v. UnumProvident Corp.*, No. 02 Civ. 8781 (DLC), 2003 WL 21997747, at *12 (S.D.N.Y. Aug. 22, 2003), http://tinyurl.com/9g8qypg] After thoroughly describing the defendant's failure to effectively communicate the need to preserve documents to IBM, the court concluded that "[i]f UnumProvident had been as diligent as it should have been in complying promptly with [the Court's prior Order], many fewer tapes would have been inadvertently overwritten." [*Id.* at *13.]

PRACTICE POINTER

Due to the evolving nature of this area of the law, and opinions suggesting that courts may become increasingly willing to impose a duty on parties to inform certain nonparties of the duty to preserve, counsel should consider issuing a litigation hold notice to third-party social media providers. A third-party notice should provide a brief synopsis of the litigation or anticipated litigation, the sender's duty to preserve, and a summary of the information sought to be preserved [See Appendix B].

Chapter Contents

Chapter 3: Discovery of Social Media Data in a Civil Action

Chapter 3

Discovery of Social Media Data in a Civil Action

1. Introduction

[3:1] **Scope of This Chapter:** The discoverability of social media data depends on the nature of the case (i.e., civil v. criminal) and whether the parties involved include the social media service provider from whom relevant data is sought. As discussed more fully below, and for ease of reference, this chapter will focus almost exclusively on the discovery of relevant social media data in a civil action *through the parties in the litigation*. In some instances the co-authors do cite to criminal cases for the limited purpose of highlighting principles expounded therein that could be applied in civil proceedings.

[3:1:1] **Discovery of Social Media Data in a Criminal Action Is Not Within the Scope of This Chapter:** This chapter does not address discovery in the context of a criminal action where specialized law and rules apply. For further insight and direction on how to seek social media data in the context of a criminal action, the authors recommend this reference: http://tinyurl.com/aajpkmp.

[3:1:2] **Discovery of Social Media Data in a Civil Action:** There are times when a social media service provider is a named party in a civil case. Generally, (assuming social media data is relevant to the claims or allegations at issue in the action), the discovery of relevant social media data from that named party social media service provider will proceed in the usual course. However, in a civil action in which neither party is the social media service provider from which data is sought, the discoverability of that data will hinge on whether *consent* to disclosure of the *relevant* private social media data has been obtained from the profile owners. After discussing why social media data is important, this chapter will discuss the applicable authorities and provides practice pointers regarding how to obtain relevant private social media data in a civil action.

2. Why Is It Important to Consider Seeking Social Media Data in Discovery?

[3:2] **People Tend to Share Information Freely on Social Media:** Regardless of how much individuals are cautioned not to send e-mails that may reflect poorly on them or their company, many people speak off the cuff and choose their words carelessly at times. People using social media speak in an even more off the cuff and uncensored manner. It is this candid dialogue that a party may want to make sure to obtain through discovery and publicly available resources and use in a case. (Fig. 3.1)

Figure 3.1   A Tweet by Will Ferrell

[3:3] **Limited Expectation of Privacy in Information on Social Media Sites:** As will be discussed more fully below, recent legal developments in the United States have expanded the scope of discovery and have re-interpreted the Fourth Amendment's "expectation of privacy." In the past few years, courts have generally disapproved of the "social network site privilege" and broadened discovery rules to include social media data *relevant*—even if "private"—to the defense or prosecution of a legal action [see *McMillen v. Hummingbird Speedway, Inc.*, No. 113 - 2010 CD, 2010 WL 4403285 (Pa. Com. Pl. Sept. 9, 2010)].

3. Obtaining Data Directly from Social Media Sites Is Problematic

[3:4] **Obstacles Encountered When Seeking Information from Service Provider:** One way to obtain relevant data is simply to request it directly from the social media service provider. However, subpoenaing information directly from a social media site is problematic for a few reasons. First, the social media service provider might fight the subpoena to protect the privacy interests of its users. Second, federal law imposes obstacles to access.

[3:4:1] **No Disclosure Without Consent:** Almost all social media service providers require a subpoena, court order, or other valid legal process to disclose information about their users. Even then, unless the subpoena is issued by law enforcement, it will likely prove difficult to obtain information via a subpoena. For example, Facebook's legal department has stated publicly that even when a subpoena is properly served, Facebook will decline to provide the user data requested. Facebook's Deputy General Counsel Mark Howitson said, "'I don't care if you snivel, the social networking site will not hand over information from a user's account to law enforcement or litigators—unless it comes after a courtroom brawl." Accordingly, Facebook's legal department is ready for a fight when user data is requested *unless that user has given his or her consent* [see Nils Victor Montan, *Facebook Legal Department not going to roll over*, http://www.ipally.com/profiles/blogs/facebook-legal-department-not (last visited Dec. 10, 2011)].

[3:4:2] **Federal Law Also Limits Disclosure Without Consent:** The U.S. Congress passed the Stored Communications Act (SCA) in 1986 as part of the Electronic Communications Privacy Act (ECPA). In general, the SCA prevents providers of communication services from divulging private communications to certain entities and individuals. The statute distinguishes between a remote computing service (RCS) provider and an electronic communications service (ECS) provider. It defines an RCS as an entity that provides to the public "computer storage or processing services by means of an electronic communications system." It defines an ECS as "any service which provides to users thereof the ability to send or receive wire or electronic communications" [see 18 U.S.C. §§ 2510(15), 2711(2)]. Although the statute was specifically enacted to deal with the advent of the Internet and "a host of potential privacy breaches that the Fourth Amendment does not address," it was adopted long before any social-networking websites had been developed. Cases interpreting the SCA are instructive, however.

[3:4:2:1] In Ninth Circuit SCA Protects Users' Confidentiality: In *Theofel v. Farey-Jones*, the Ninth Circuit disapproved of a subpoena for "all e-mails sent or received by anyone" at the plaintiff's company on the ground of over-breadth pursuant to Rule 45. A panel of the Ninth Circuit Court of Appeals reversed the trial courts dismissal of the plaintiff's SCA claim against its Internet service provider (ISP), which had responded to the subpoena. Judge Alex Kozinski wrote that the Act "reflects Congress's judgment that users have a legitimate interest in the confidentiality of communications in electronic storage at a communications facility." He concluded that because the overbroad subpoena "transparently and egregiously" violated the federal rules, the ISP's production of e-mails created a cognizable claim under the Act. [*Theofel v. Farey-Jones*, 359 F.3d 1066, 1071 (9th Cir. 2004), http://tinyurl.com/9zu7ygk]

[3:4:2:2] California Federal Court Finds Social Networking Sites Protected by SCA: In *Crispin v. Christian Audigier*, a federal court in the Central District of California quashed subpoenas to Myspace and Facebook on the grounds that some of the content on those sites is protected by the SCA, and because the user had selected certain privacy settings intended to limit access to his pages. [*Crispin v. Christian Audigier, Inc.*, No. 09-09509, 2010 WL 2293238 (C.D. Cal. May 26, 2010) (unpublished decision), http://tinyurl.com/8sfz4p3] The plaintiff artist alleged that the defendants used his artwork in violation of their oral agreement, and he filed suit for copyright infringement. The court held that private messaging and e-mail services provided by social networking sites constitute ECS, and that such sites are both ECS and RCS providers as to wall postings and comments posted on an account holder's Web page. The court concluded that webmail and private messaging services provided on social-networking websites are not subject to subpoena under the SCA, because such messages were not readily accessible to the general public and were, therefore, inherently private. (As to wall postings and comments, the court punted by sending the case back to the trial court and stating that it needed more of an evidentiary record to determine whether they were "inherently private" and therefore protected from disclosure by the SCA). As of the date of publication, no new opinion is available regarding this court's eventual evaluation of this issue.

Strongly Criticized: The decision has been harshly criticized as applying "outmoded federal electronic privacy laws from the 1980s" to "new technologies." [Alan Klein *et al.*, *Social Networking Sites: Subject to Discovery? Ruling Holds that Messages and Comments Visible to a Restricted Set of Users Are Protected*, Nat'l L.J. 15, Aug. 23, 2010.] One article points out that computer use has changed dramatically since 1986, when subscribers used third-party network services for two main purposes: "sending communications, such as e-mail, and outsourcing resource-intensive computing tasks, such as storing large files or processing data." [*Id.*] The authors state that the definitions of the SCA and ECPA do not readily fit the capabilities of social-networking sites. Moreover, the authors point out that the decision does not address "how restricted access to content must be in order for that content to be considered private, [and] the interaction between a provider's policies and an individual's privacy choices." [*Id.*] To date, these questions have been left undecided by the entirety of applicable jurisprudence.

[3:4:2:3] **Workers Compensation Commission Finds ECPA Protects Users' Social Media Data:** In 2009, the Virginia Workers' Compensation Commission relied on the ECPA to limit discovery of social networking site information. In September 2009, Facebook fought a subpoena issued in a Virginia Workers' compensation case that sought photographs posted by the claimant. The employer hoped the photographs would demonstrate that the claimant's alleged back injury was not as serious as claimed. The deputy commissioner agreed that pursuant to the ECPA [18 U.S.C. §§ 2510 *et seq.*] the claimant's "privacy decision" must be respected and could be enforced by Facebook to protect its user's data.

> **PRACTICE POINTER**
>
> Discovery requests and trial subpoenas served directly on social media sites will likely be met with objections or even a non-response as courts are not likely to force social media sites to respond to the subpoena in a civil action unless the party to the action has given consent. In light of this, the remainder of this chapter will focus on the applicable authorities, which support seeking relevant data (1) through the parties in the litigation via formal discovery and (2) via informal means.

4. Obtaining Social Media Evidence Via Formal Discovery Through a Party to the Litigation.

[3:5] **Court Ordered Consent**: If a defendant cannot get the plaintiff to voluntarily agree to provide written consent, courts will most likely require a plaintiff to provide signed authorizations for the production of relevant social media discovery. In *McMillen v. Hummingbird Speedway, Inc.*, 2010 WL 4403285 (C.P. Jefferson Sept. 9, 2010) [http://tinyurl.com/3dz5mhl], the defendant race track company demanded that the plaintiff, an injured stock car driver, produce his Facebook login information to allow for inspection of his profile. The judge rejected the plaintiff's argument that social media postings were privileged and confidential, ordering the plaintiff to produce the password and allow access for fifteen days. [*Id.* at *8. See also *Largent v. Reed*, No. 2009-1823, 2011 WL 5632688 (Pa. Franklin C.P. 11/08/2011)]. The plaintiff did not object on the basis that the request was overly broad, an argument other courts have embraced to reject access to an entire account.

PRACTICE POINTER

A Consent Agreement for Social Media documents can be reached the same way any consent agreement between parties can be reached. One method is to call opposing counsel and discuss the matter with him or her. Thereafter, simply forward a draft consent letter to opposing counsel. A copy of the draft consent letter can also be included in discovery requests.

Even though there are no magic words and the Consent Agreement can be basic, there are three primary areas you want to ensure are included. (1) *Background information:* user name, password, e-mail address, birth date, URL for profile, address, and full name of user; (2) *Document requests:* any and all communications—i.e., wall posts, e-mails, photographs, deleted e-mails, postings, friend lists, etc.; (3) *Indemnity:* Facebook, Twitter, Myspace and others have typically required that a party agree to indemnify them before they will produce the records.

If a party includes the foregoing in their consent request, the social media provider will typically produce the requested documents. Please note, however, that some social media providers, such as Myspace, require a subpoena along with the executed consent agreement. Others have required a Court Order along with the consent agreement. As each provider is unique, a party should consult the provider's user services page before submitting the paperwork. [e.g., www.facebook.com/legal/terms]

[3:6] **According to the Federal Rules, No Privacy Exception Can Exist in Social Media Content:** The Federal Rules, and equivalent state rules, do not recognize any "privacy" exception to the requirements of discovery (much less a "social networking privacy" exception) [see Fed. R. Civ. P. 33 advisory committee's note referencing "sensitive interests of confidentiality or privacy" in responding to certain interrogatories but not suggesting a general privacy exception. Similar (limited) notes appear in regard to Rules 34 and 45. See *id.* 34, 45].

[3:7] **"Very Nature and Purpose" of Social Media Is to Share Personal Information:** "[W]hen Plaintiff created her Facebook and Myspace accounts, she consented to the fact that her personal information would be shared with others, notwithstanding her privacy settings. Indeed, that is the very nature and purpose of these social networking sites else they would cease to exist .... [I]n this environment, privacy is no longer grounded in reasonable expectations, but rather in some theoretical protocol better known as wishful thinking." [*Romano*, 907 N.Y.S.2d at 657.]

[3:7:1] **Very Public Forum:** On Facebook, for example, a setting many might consider as a "private" setting is "friends only." Yet the average Facebook user has 130 "friends," who could share posted information with their "friends," and "friends" of "friends," on so on. [http://tinyurl.com/35c7fmq] Nevertheless, social media users tend to post highly personal, and oftentimes embarrassing, information [e.g., *Simply Storage Mgmt., LLC*, 270 F.R.D. at 434; *Ledbetter v. Wal-Mart Stores, Inc.*, No. 06-cv-01958-WYD-MJW, 2009 WL 1067018 (D. Colo. Apr. 21, 2009), http://tinyurl.com/9r74bkn] (Fig. 3.2).

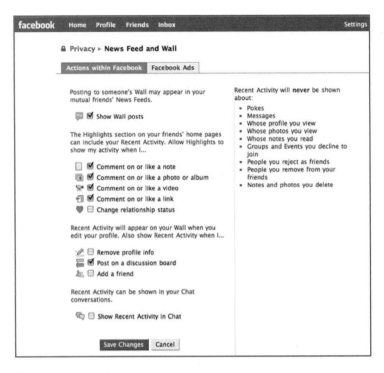

Figure 3.2   Facebook Privacy Page

[3:8] **No Fishing Expeditions—Party Cannot "Fish" for Information on Profiles:** Courts have held that pure fishing expeditions are not permitted and have required a preliminary showing of relevance before ordering broad social media discovery. For example, in *Abrams v. Pecile*, 83 A.D.3d 527 (1st Dept 2011) [http://tinyurl.com/8pzoy72], the plaintiff filed suit seeking damages for, among other things, conversion and intentional infliction of emotional distress arising from the defendant's alleged unauthorized possession of seminude photographs of the plaintiff. In her demand for discovery, the defendant sought access to the plaintiff's social networking accounts and the trial court ordered the plaintiff to comply with that request. On appeal, the First Department disagreed, concluding that the defendant failed to show that permitting access would lead to the discovery of evidence relevant to the defense of the lawsuit: "(The defendant has made) no showing ... that 'the method of discovery sought will result in the disclosure of relevant evidence or is reasonably calculated to lead to the discovery of information bearing on the claims' .... Because plaintiff admits that she has copies of the photographs contained on the subject CD, defendant has also failed to show that she needs access to plaintiff's hard drive in order to defeat plaintiff's conversion claim." [*Id.;* see also *McCann v. Harleysville Ins. Co. of N.Y.,* 910 N.Y.S.2d 614, 615 (2010); *Munis v. United Parcel Serv., Inc.,* No. C-09-01987-CW (DMR), 2011 WL 311374, at *8 (N.D. Cal. Jan. 28, 2011), http://tinyurl.com/8tluvyd] Sections 3:17 through 3:19 provide several examples:

[3:8:1] Discoverable Where Social Media Data Is "Material and Necessary" for Party's Defense: In *Romano v. Steelcase, Inc.,* the defendant sought an order granting Defendant access to Plaintiff's current and historical Facebook and Myspace pages and accounts, including all deleted pages and related information upon the grounds that Plaintiff placed certain information on the social networking sites that was believed to be inconsistent with her personal injury claims. [*Romano v. Steelcase, Inc.,* 907 N.Y.S.2d 650, 654 (N.Y. Sup. Ct. 2010).] The court granted Defendant's access to the plaintiff's social media data reasoning, "[t]he information sought by Defendant regarding Plaintiff's Facebook and Myspace accounts is both material and necessary to the defense of this action and/or could lead to admissible evidence," and "Defendant's need for access to the information outweighs any privacy concerns that may be voiced by Plaintiff." [*Id.* at 657.] As a result, Defendant relied on Plaintiff's smiling Facebook photos to refute allegations that her injuries confined her to her house and bed.

[3:8:2] Discoverable Where Emotional or Mental State Is at Issue in Action: In *EEOC v. Simply Storage Management,* a sexual harassment case where claimants alleged extreme emotional distress, the court allowed discovery into claimants' Facebook and Myspace "profiles, postings, or messages (including status updates, wall comments, causes joined, groups joined, activity streams, blog entries) and [social network site] applications [for the relevant period] that reveal, refer, or relate to any emotion, feeling, or mental state," as well as communications that refer to events that "could reasonably be expected to produce a significant emotion, feeling, or mental state." [*EEOC v. Simply Storage Mgmt., LLC*, 270 F.R.D. 430, 436 (S.D. Ind. 2010).] The court ordered such discovery regardless of whether these materials were designated "private" by claimants on their Facebook and Myspace accounts, reasoning that a basic protective order would suffice to address any privacy concerns. The court observed: "It is reasonable to expect severe emotional or mental injury to manifest itself in some [social media] content, and an examination of that content might reveal whether onset occurred, when, and the degree of distress. Further, information that evidences other stressors that could have produced the alleged emotional distress is also relevant." [*Id.* at 435.] The court also ordered discovery of photos and videos that related to claimant's emotions, feelings, and mental states.

[3:8:3] **Discoverable Where Party Waives Right to Privacy:** Similarly, a family court permitted a father to use the mother's Myspace writings to establish her sado-masochism, bisexuality, pagan tendencies, and illicit drug use to help win custody of his child. [*Dexter v. Dexter*, No. 2006-P-0051, 2007 WL 1532084, at *6 (Ohio App. May 25, 2007).] The court reasoned, "with respect to her Myspace account, appellant admitted in open court that she wrote these on-line blogs and that these writings were open to the public to view. Thus, she can hardly claim an expectation of privacy regarding these writings." [*Id.* at *6 n.4.]

[3:8:4] **Discoverable Where Social Media Data Can Impeach a Witness:** In an Arizona criminal case, the government used Defendant's Myspace profile to prove his Internet usage and alcohol consumption in violation of his probation. On appeal, Defendant argued that the trial court erred in admitting the photographs. The appellate court found the trial court did not abuse its discretion in admitting the photographs because they were relevant to whether or not Defendant violated the term of probation and were introduced on cross-examination to impeach witness' testimony. [*Arizona v. Pressley*, No. 1CA-CR-08-0160, 2009 WL 2343139, at *3 (Ariz. Ct. App. 2009) (non-precedential mem. disp.)]

PRACTICE POINTER

From these cases we can glean the following:

Subject Placed at Issue: Courts are routinely holding that the defendant's need for access to the social media data outweighs any of the plaintiff's privacy concerns when the social media data is material and relevant to the defense or prosecution of a cause of action. The party seeking discovery must establish that the plaintiff has put some subject at issue to which social media content may be relevant.

Additional Evidence Exists: In many cases, the party seeking the discovery must produce some evidence establishing that there is likely *additional* relevant evidence contained within the social media profiles. Where there is some evidence available that tends to show that there may be more discoverable information contained within the private or otherwise unavailable portions of a party's account, a court is more likely to allow social media discovery to occur.

Narrow Discovery Requests: The defendant must draft the discovery request as narrowly as possible. It appears that the scope of a permissible discovery request will be a fact-specific inquiry and will likely be determined on a case-by-case basis. When the relevancy of the discovery is questionable to start with, the court is much less likely to allow extremely broad discovery requests, such as those requesting the entire contents of certain social media applications. Where, however, the discovery can be shown to be relevant or reasonably calculated to lead to potentially relevant material, the courts will likely be more willing to allow for a broader scope of discovery.

[See Appendix A for sample discovery requests.]

Definitions: One easy method of including social media in discovery requests is to add social media accounts or profiles to the (often boilerplate) definition of "document" in such requests. While at least one court has construed "profile" broadly [*Simply Storage Mgmt., LLC,* 270 F.R.D. at 432 n.1], it may be better to include expressly all postings, profiles, walls, comments, pictures, videos, blogs, messages, and other sources of social media information likely to contain relevant information. In *Simply Storage Management,* the court reproduced the requests at issue, and those requests provide a helpful model. [*Id.* at 432.] (See Appendix A for the author's sample discovery requests, which are similar to the requests reproduced in Simply Storage Mgmt.)

Monitoring Software: Written discovery requests should also target a company's access to data that may establish knowledge of a product defect or violation. For example, a corporation's monitoring software (e.g., Alterian SM2, Lithium or Radian 6, which have the ability to monitor publicly accessible blog posts and comments, Twitter feeds, Facebook profiles, Flickr, and many other social media providers regarding conversations surrounding a brand and aggregate the results into positive and negative categories for quick review) provides a potential opportunity to argue that the company received notice of almost any customer problem mentioned on the Internet. Take a product liability case as an example. In the past, the plaintiff in a products liability case might have conducted extensive discovery about customer complaints that the company received for a particular product. However, just as the majority of dissatisfied diners leave a restaurant without voicing a complaint, the majority of upset customers do not make a formal complaint with a manufacturer. A very large number of people, however, may tell their story in a blog or in a posting on a social media website. Through monitoring software, a corporation may receive a notification or summary of these discussions on the Internet. By requesting information relating to such monitoring software and the related notifications, a party may be able to show that the company had notice of a wide variety of complaints made on the Internet, and perhaps even adopted a social media strategy to try to counteract such complaints.

Waiver: If the opposing party has posted comments to its social media account (e.g., Facebook) or to a blog that concerns conversations with its legal counsel about developments in its litigation, a discovery request for these communications should be served on the grounds that the party has waived any attorney-client privilege. In *Lenz v. Universal Music Corp.*, No. C 07-03783 JF (PVT), 2010 WL 4286329 (N.D. Cal. Oct. 22, 2010), http://tinyurl.com/8mjd8eh, for example, the U.S. District Court for the Northern District of California ordered disclosure of some otherwise privileged communications in a case in which the plaintiff discussed the case and discussions with her legal counsel on her blog site and in Gmail chats with her friend.

5. Obtaining Social Media Data Via Informal Discovery Tactics and the Corresponding Ethical Issues to Consider

[3:9] **Do Not Overlook Potentially Relevant Evidence Available Publicly, but Be Aware of Ethical Considerations:** It is not always necessary to rely exclusively on formal discovery to obtain relevant information. At times, it may be fruitful and cost effective to also seek evidence informally via publicly available sources. This section discusses these sources and the ethical issues that apply.

[3:10] **Freely Accessible Public Portion of a Party's Social Media Profile:** An attorney may freely review and access any public portions of the social media profiles of an adverse party [e.g., N.Y. Comm. On Prof'l Ethics, Op. 843 (Sept. 2010) http://tinyurl.com/9pjzyzr]. Of course, an attorney does well to become acquainted with and not violate applicable ethical rules [*see* [3:25] and [3:28] for an ethics considerations].

[3:10:1] **However, Do Not "Friend" a Represented Adverse Party:** However, to "friend" a represented adverse party is likely to run afoul of applicable ethical rules. For example, Arizona's ethical rules "prohibit a lawyer … from communicating about the subject of the representation with a party if the lawyer knows that the party is represented by another lawyer in the matter, unless the lawyer has the other lawyer's consent or is otherwise authorized by law to do so." [Ariz. R. S. Ct. 42, Ethical Rule 4.2 (Communication with Person Represented by Counsel).] Rule 4.2 does not expressly address communications with a represented adverse party via social media. Nevertheless, it is the course of wisdom to avoid communicating with a represented adverse party via social media in much the same way an attorney would avoid doing so in the real world.

> **PRACTICE POINTER**
>
> Because some social media is a steady stream of information that is not easily captured and preserved, it is worth setting up a system to monitor the usage of social media that is publicly available from the beginning of any litigation. This system should include the other party, key witnesses for that party, and experts once they have been identified [see [3:25] and [3:28] for ethics considerations]. One possible approach is to assign a paralegal or associate to go online every day and view the user's usage [see [4:3] and [4:4]].

[3:11] **"Friending" a Judge, Witness, or Unrepresented Party:** Whether a judge may "friend" an attorney, or whether an

attorney may "friend" a witness or an unrepresented party—
or direct another to do so on his or her behalf—is less clear.
Judges and attorneys must be careful when trying to obtain
non-public information from private social media sites as
they can run afoul of ethical rules or ethical opinions if they
directly or indirectly use deceptive means to obtain access to
the information. Several state ethics committees have issued
opinions relevant to these issues:

[3:11:1] **Judges and Lawyers Should Not "Friend" Each Other:**
The Florida Judicial Ethics Committee recently issued an advisory opinion stating that judges may not "add lawyers who
appear before them as 'friends' on a social networking site,
[or] permit such lawyers to add the judge as their 'friend.'"

[3:11:2] **Split on Whether to "Friend" Unrepresented Party:**

[3:11:2:1] **New York City Bar:** The New York City Bar, for example, has opined that an attorney may engage in the truthful,
non-deceptive "friending" of unrepresented persons. [N.Y.C.
Comm. on Prof. & Jud. Ethics, Formal Op. 2010-2, "Obtaining
Evidence from Social Networking Sites" (Sept. 2010).] The New
York City Bar endorses this approach so long as the lawyer or
agent does not engage "in the direct or indirect use of affirmatively 'deceptive' behavior" to "friend" the witness, such as
creating a fraudulent profile that falsely portrays the lawyer
or agent as a long-lost classmate, a prospective employer or a
friend of a friend. Of course, the attorney has an ethical obligation to disclose his or her real name.

[3:11:2:2] **Philadelphia Bar:** In contrast, the Philadelphia Bar
Association Professional Guidance Committee has declared
that an attorney may not "friend," directly or via an agent, an
unrepresented person whom the other side intends to call as
witness without revealing that the lawyer is seeking information for possible use antagonistic to the witness. Even if the

attorney (or paralegal) had provided his or her real name, the Philadelphia Bar, unlike the NYC Bar, still held this to be unethical. [Phila. Prof. Guidance Comm., Op. 2009-02 (Mar. 2009).] The committee reasoned that the omission of the attorney's intent to obtain impeachment information from the witness's social media accounts would be deceptive and violate Ethical Rules 4.1 and 8.4. The committee found it of no significance that the witness grants "friend requests" as a matter of course and therefore exposes herself or himself to such risks.

[3:12] **Freely Accessible, Publicly Available Data on Judges and Attorneys:** Social media research on judges, lawyers, and experts is not strictly related to social media as evidence, but it is important to consider because this type of data may be important to a case. The following are a few examples:

[3:12:1] **Freely Accessible, Publicly Available Data on Lawyers:** Many freely accessible sites contain publicly available data on attorneys. Good social media sites to look at in researching lawyers include LinkedIn.com, 123people.com, and avvo.com, in addition to traditional Internet tools, such as firm websites, bar associations, and martindale.com. It may be possible to learn whether an attorney has expertise in a certain area of the law, how often he or she has appeared before the assigned judge, whether he or she settles most cases or wins them on motions or takes them to trial. This information could help attorneys better understand an opponent or make the best choice in selecting local counsel.

[3:12:2] **Freely Accessible, Publicly Available Data on Judges:** Attorneys should check to see if the trial judge posts on a blog and what subjects he or she may be writing on. It is worth knowing if the judge is connected with any party or witnesses in the upcoming trial. The same is true for cases in arbitration and the arbitrator(s). This information could help attorneys understand a judge's experiences or expertise in particular areas of law, interactions with opposing counsel, biases, and tendencies, such as citing unpublished opinions, in order to help develop strategy and better advise clients about what to expect.

[3:12:2:1] **Growing Number of Judges Are Maintaining Social Networking Profiles:** Counsel should always be interested in learning the leanings of the Court and/or whether there is anything in the judge's background that disqualifies the Court for hearing a particular case. Toward this end, a growing number of judges maintain profiles on social networking sites, including Richard Clifton of Ninth Circuit, John M. Ferren of the D.C. Circuit, Deborah Cook of the Sixth Circuit, and Jennifer Elrod and Edith Jones of the Fifth Circuit. Litigants should vet a judge's social networking profile in advance of trial. Even some courts can be found on social media sites. For example, the New Jersey Judiciary announced in September 2009 that they will use Twitter, Facebook, and YouTube to provide breaking court news, closings, lawyer volunteer opportunities, and the like. Users can sign up to get news alerts from the court and court-sent Tweets on their cell phones.

[3:12:2:2] **At Least One Judge Maintained a Personal Website, Which Became Publicly Available:** In the Ninth Circuit, the Honorable Alex Kozinski was in the middle of an obscenity trial when the *Los Angeles Times* broke a story that he had an extensive collection of suggestive or explicit images and videos on his personal website, which had become publicly available. Judge Kozinski disqualified himself from hearing the obscenity case. Judge Kozinski also declared a mistrial in the case. The newspaper story had raised a suspicion that the court could be biased in favor of the defendants. (Fig. 3.3)

Judge Kozinski admonished for explicit items on Web site

July 02, 2009 | By Bill Mears CNN

Share   Twitter   Email

Recommend   Be the first of your friends to recommend this.

A judicial council on Thursday admonished the chief judge of the nation's largest federal appeals court for having "sexually explicit photos and videos" on his personal Web site, but decided against any further punishment.

Judge Alex Kozinski, 58, of the San Francisco, California-based 9th Circuit U.S. Court of Appeals previously apologized and had recommended an investigation because of the public controversy over the material.

The panel chose not to discipline Judge Alex Kozinski beyond the admonishment.

A panel of judges assigned to investigate concluded Kozinski's "possession of sexually explicit offensive material combined with his carelessness in failing to safeguard his sphere of privacy was judicially imprudent." His actions, the panel wrote, "can reasonably be seen as having resulted in embarrassment to the institution of the federal judiciary."

Figure 3.3   Screenshot of Judge Kozinski Article

PRACTICE POINTER

A judge may have a hard time distancing himself or herself from posts that reflect personal biases or opinions on matters that are being litigated in his or her courtroom. This is not to suggest that the judge will necessarily recuse himself or herself as Judge Kozinski did in the obscenity trial. However, it is information that an attorney should seek out as part of the normal due diligence that is done when a case is assigned to a judge.

---

6. Obtaining Social Media Data from Expert Witnesses

[3:13] **Check Blogs and Social Media Sites:** People are branding themselves as knowledge leaders through blog sites and social media posts. The same will be true for many expert witnesses who will testify at trial. Before designating your own experts, be sure to do your due diligence on what they have written in the past on social media in connection with your client, its industry, and also the issues for which the witness is being asked to testify. If there are any red flags, you want to know sooner rather than later.

PRACTICE POINTER

You may want to include in the experts' engagement letter that they will not discuss the case on social media or blog sites until the case is completely over, including any appeals, and, further, that anything discussed with the client or its counsel during the case that did not come out through trial is confidential and should never be disclosed.

[3:14] **Experts Are Relying on Blogs More and More:** Courts are now citing to blog posts in their opinions [see, e.g., *United States v. Everett III*, 601 F.3d 484, 493 (6th Cir. 2010), http://tinyurl.com/94ynm9y]. In *Everett III*, a case involving, *inter alia*, a felony conviction for possession of a firearm, which Everett volunteered during a routine traffic stop, the court addressed whether case precedent imposed a categorical ban on questioning that is unrelated and without suspicion and which may minimally prolong a traffic stop. In answering this question in the negative, the *Everett* court cited and relied upon commentary in online blogs. *[Id.]* There is an increasing trend for court clerks to use blogs as a source for researching legal issues in the same way that they have used law review comments in the past. In a speech on August 19, 2010, Justice Anthony Kennedy gave made a passing comment that law review case comments usually come out too late to be of use to the Court, so he finds his clerks are reading blogs in interesting cases. [http://tinyurl.com/9e69lus]

PRACTICE POINTER

Formal Discovery Requests: Through pre-trial discovery, the other side's expert should be asked to identify the social media on which the expert has posted and to produce copies of those posts.

Deposition: Further, a standard deposition question should be what blog sites the expert subscribes to. Additionally, there should be follow-up questions to develop areas for cross-examination. Counsel also should try to have the expert in his deposition validate other blog sites as accepted authorities in their respective field.

Impeachment: This social media discovery can be used for impeaching the expert at trial. It also is a helpful resource for identifying other experts in the area who may have blog posts that counsel should offer as a "learned treatise" for impeachment of the expert pursuant to Rule 803(18) of the Federal Rules of Evidence.

Chapter Contents

Chapter 4: Foundation and Authentication

Chapter 4

Foundation and Authentication

1. Introduction

[4:1] **The Challenge—Tracking the Source of Social Media Data:** People can use pseudonyms on social media. In addition, it can be difficult to show a clear path from the person to the social media post and, thereby, demonstrate the preliminary fact that the statement was made by the witness. Information found on social media sites is susceptible to fraud and manipulation. [*Griffin v. Maryland*, 19 A.3d 415, 426 (Md. App. Ct. 2011).] Sometimes there is a problem with viruses and spam messages from "friends" as a result of Internet hacking. A party who is opposing introduction of the evidence can cite to these recognized problems to challenge whether the social media statement was made by the witness. Social media also is accessible through passwords that may have been shared by the alleged speaker, or the computer and social networking site may have been left logged on so anyone with access to the computer could have posted the statements. Not surprisingly, courts have recognized that electronically stored information "may require greater scrutiny than that required for the authentication of 'hard copy' documents." [*Lorraine v. Markel Am. Ins. Co.*, 241 F.R.D. 534, 542-43 (D. Md. 2007).] (Fig. 4.1)

[4:2] **The Challenge—Collecting and Preserving Social Media Data:** Given the transient and cloud-based nature of social media data, it generally cannot be collected and preserved by traditional computer forensics tools and processes. Full disk images of computers in the cloud is effectively impossible, and the industry has lacked tools designed to collect social media items in a scalable manner while supporting litigation requirements, such as the capture and preservation of all key metadata, read only access, and the generation of hash values and chain of custody. (Hash values are used to identify and filter duplicate files (e.g., e-mail, attachments, and loose files) from an ESI collection or verify that a forensic image or clone was captured successfully.) In fact, the proper and timely preservation of social media evidence is a major concern, with courts finding spoliation [*Katiroll Co., Inc. v. Kati Roll & Platters, Inc.*, No. 10-3620 (GEB), 2011 WL 3583408 (D.N.J. Aug. 3, 2011), http://tinyurl.com/8t6m52t] or otherwise mandating preservation by the individual account owner's in recent cases. [*EEOC v. Simply Storage Mgmt.*, 270 F.R.D. 430 (S.D. Ind. May 11, 2010).] Once preserved, discovery protocols and authentication are disjointed, with courts themselves reviewing Facebook accounts in some instances. [*Offenback v. L.M. Bowman, Inc.*, No. 1:10-CV-1789, 2011 WL 2491371 (M.D. Pa. June 22, 2011), http://tinyurl.com/97qojnp] In one case, a trial judge resorted to personally friending a witness on Facebook in order to authenticate the witness' postings on the site. [*Barnes* *v. CUS Nashville, LLC*, No. 3:09-cv-00764, 2010 WL 2265668 (M.D. Tenn. June 3, 2010), http://tinyurl.com/999cd3e]

[4:2:1] **Ad Hoc Collection and Preservation Measures Are Deficient:** When seeking to collect social media data either for your own review, use, and preservation or for production to the opposing party, *ad hoc* collection and preservation measures are deficient. Many *ad hoc* measures currently used to collect social media for use in court do not meet the authentication and admissibility requirements. Screen capture tools (e.g., Snipping Tool, FastStone Capture, Jing, or Skitch) and many archive services (e.g., Iron Mountain) fail to collect most available metadata or generate hash values needed for tracking and identification for individual social media items upon collection.

[See *Practice Pointer* under [2.2] for a discussion on what to look out for when thinking about and preparing for how to collect social media data.]

[4:2:2] **Self-Collection Is Similarly Deficient:** The Facebook self-collection mechanism currently will not collect most available metadata information, will not generate hash values, and will only provide content from the user's own account while omitting content contributed by that user to their friend's account, such as to their friend's "walls." eDiscovery leader KMPG provided a written release noting that the Facebook download feature "was not conceived to be a forensic collection tool. The only original timestamps that it preserves are in the HTML files which can be easily modified." There currently is no self-collection or even an export feature for Twitter, LinkedIn, Myspace or other social media sites.

> **PRACTICE POINTER**
>
> Companies should work with legal counsel and their IT/litigation support departments—prior to any litigation—to identify the best venders for their helping them to retain and collect their electronically stored data. Some terms worth negotiating with the vendor include: (1) spelling out whether the vendor will or will not have ownership over the collected data; (2) strict limitations on who can have access to the data such as senior IT personnel at the company; (3) the retention period for the data; and (4) storing personal data in encrypted form.

2. The Foundational Requirement for Use of Evidence

[4:3] **The Rules of Evidence Focus on Relevance:** The Rules of Evidence govern the admissibility of social media as evidence. For example, under the Federal Rules of Evidence, the trial attorney will have to meet the requirements of Rule 401 by demonstrating that the social media evidence has the "tendency to make the existence of a fact … more probable or less probable than it would be without the evidence" (i.e., social media evidence must have a purpose). Similarly, under Rule 403, the probative value must outweigh the danger of unfair prejudice, confusion, misleading of jury (e.g., an entire Facebook page may not be admissible, but only relevant portions). In addition, witness statements on social media sites may be hearsay, but multiple exceptions could apply, such as an admission by party-opponent, admissible under Rule 801(d)(2) or present sense impression of the witness, admissible under Rule 803(1). Of course, A third-party "wall posting" or a responsive "comment" sought to be introduced into evidence will probably be deemed inadmissible hearsay.

[4:4] **Standard for Authentication Is Relatively Low:** The standard for authentication is relatively low [see Fed. R. Evid. 901(a)]. Under Federal Rule Evidence 901(a), a proponent of evidence at trial must offer "evidence sufficient to support a finding that the matter in question is what its proponent claims." Unless uncontroverted and cooperative witness testimony is available, the proponent must rely on other means to establish a proper foundation. A party can authenticate electronically stored information per Rule 901(b)(4) with circumstantial evidence that reflects the "contents, substance, internal patterns, or other distinctive characteristics" of the evidence.

[4:4:1] **Circumstantial Evidence:** In the context of e-mails and text messages, courts have admitted the evidence based on circumstantial evidence, and allowed the jury based on the parties' testimony and arguments to decide how much weight to put on the evidence. In *Lorraine v. Markel Am. Ins. Co.*, 241 F.R.D. 534, 542-43 (D. Md. 2007), for example, the court noted that similar uncertainties exist with traditional written documents with signatures that can be forged, or distinctive letterhead stationary that can be copied or stolen. These kinds of arguments might also be applied to social media data:

[4:4:1:1] **Dates and Presence of Identifying Web Address Used to Authenticate Social Media Data:** In ruling on a motion for preliminary injunction, in *Perfect 10, Inc. v. Cybernet Ventures, Inc.*, 213 F. Supp. 2d 1146, 1153-54 (C.D. Cal. 2002), http://tinyurl.com/94c46mc, the court overruled objections made to exhibits printed from the Internet that were printed by a party representative who attached the exhibits to his declaration. The court found that the dates and web addresses from which the images were printed provided "circumstantial indicia of authenticity," which, together with the declaration, would support a reasonable juror in the belief that the documents were what Plaintiff said they were. (The court also noted a reduced evidentiary standard in preliminary injunction motions.)

[4:4:1:2] **Receipt of Data, Knowledge of its Content, and Responsive Reply May Serve as Basis for Authentication:** In *United States v. Siddiqui*, 235 F.3d 1318, 1322 (11th Cir. 2000), http://tinyurl.com/8kmk4n4, the Eleventh Circuit court allowed the government to authenticate certain e-mails solely through the use of circumstantial evidence, such as the e-mail's own distinctive characteristics and the circumstances surrounding its discovery. In particular, the court found that the e-mail was properly authenticated as having been authored by Defendant because it bore Defendant's e-mail address, a reply was directed automatically to Defendant's e-mail address, and the content of the e-mail referred to matters known to Defendant.

[4:4:1:3] **"The Characteristics of the Offered Item Itself":**

[4:4:1:3:1] *Griffin v. Maryland*, **19 A.3d 415 (Md. App. Ct. 2011):** the Court of Appeals of Maryland ordered re-trial of a criminal conviction based solely on the state's failure to properly authenticate Myspace pages used during trial. *Griffin*, along with the other cases relied on by the court in reaching its decision, brings attention to the critical issue of the authentication and admissibility of SNS content at trial. The defendant in Griffin was charged with and convicted of second degree murder, assault, and illegal use of a handgun, for which he was sentenced to 50 years in prison. [*Griffin v. Maryland*, 995 A.2d 791, 794 (Md. Ct. Spec. App. 2010)]. The defendant appealed his conviction, arguing that the trial court abused its discretion by admitting hard-copy printouts of Myspace pages into evidence without proper authentication. [*Id.* at 799.] The pages, allegedly printed from the defendant's girlfriend's Myspace profile page, were offered to demonstrate that she had threatened a witness prior to the trial. [*Id.* at 796.] The pages were listed under a pseudonym but contained a number of facts identifying the girlfriend, such as her age, hometown and birth date. [*Id.* at 796, 806.] The pages also included a photograph next to the user's description of a couple embracing, which both the court and counsel agreed looked like the defendant and his girlfriend. [*Id.* at 796.] A posting on the profile was included among the Myspace pages, in which the author suggested that anyone who "SNITCHES GET STITCHES!! U KNOW WHO YOU ARE!!" [*Id.* at 795.] The prosecutors authenticated the pages through the testimony of the lead investigator on the case and did not ask the girlfriend about them. [*Id.* at 796-97.]

On appeal, the defendant objected that "the State had not sufficiently established a connection" between the defendant's girlfriend and the Myspace pages. [*Id.* at 796.] The intermediate appellate court disagreed and concluded that the trial court did not abuse its discretion in admitting the Myspace pages because the testimony of the lead investigator and circumstantial evidence, such as content and context of the pictures and postings, properly authenticated the profile as belonging to her. [*Id.* at 806-807.]

The Maryland Court of Appeals reversed this holding, finding instead that the trial court had abused its discretion because the picture and personal information used to authenticate the pictures "were not sufficient 'distinctive characteristics'" to authenticate the pages. The court first observed that while Myspace typically requires a unique username and password to establish a profile and access, friends of the user may freely post to the site. Therefore, the "identity of who generated the profile may be confound[ed], because 'a person observing the online profile of a user with whom the observer is unacquainted has no idea whether the profile is legitimate.'"

[4:4:1:3:2] **Conversely, *Tienda v. State*, No. 05-09-00553-CR, 2010 Tex. App. LEXIS 10031 (Tex. App. –Dallas Dec. 17, 2010):** the Dallas Court of Appeals applied a relatively lenient standard for admitting photographs found on a defendant's Myspace profile. In *Tienda*, a defendant was charged with murder in a gang-related drive-by shooting. The prosecution introduced several photographs that were allegedly found on the defendant's Myspace profile, with the caption, "*If you ain't blasting, you ain't lasting,*" and the notation, "*Rest in peace, David Valadez,*" which was the name of the deceased victim. [*Id.* at *8.] Another photograph offered by the prosecution was of the defendant displaying his electronic monitor (which he was required to wear as a condition of bond), stating "srt8 outta jail and n da club." [*Id.* at *8-9.] The prosecution laid the foundation for these pictures through the testimony of the victim's sister, who testified that she found them on Myspace. The trial court admitted the evidence over the defendant's objection that the prosecution had failed to authenticate the profile.

In concluding that the trial court did not abuse its discretion in admitting the Myspace evidence, the court of appeal noted that (1) the Myspace evidence was registered to a person with the defendant's nickname and legal name, (2) the photographs on the profiles were clearly of the defendant, and (3) the profile referenced the victim's murder and the defendant being arrested and placed on electronic monitoring. [*Id.* at *12.] The court stated, "[t]his type of individualization is significant in authenticating a particular profile page as having been created by the person depicted in it. The more particular and individualized the information, the greater the support for a reasonable juror's finding that the person depicted supplied the information." [*Id.*]

[4:4:1:3:3] **What to Do?:** While the courts' analysis of the authentication of SNS-based evidence concerned criminal matters, the reasoning in these two cases provides both criminal and civil litigants with important guidance regarding the evidentiary issues surrounding social networking content. To be sure, the *Griffin* decision may set the bar too high for authentication of social media evidence, but the case has not been overturned. So for now, we can safely say that there are at least three three methods by which SNS evidence could be properly authenticated even in the face of the *Griffin* decision:

First, deposition testimony from the creator or author that attests to the authenticity of the SNS submissions. [*Id.*] Although a criminal Defendant would not be obligated to testify pursuant to the Fifth Amendment, civil proceedings provide for the admission of this testimony. Therefore, litigants ought to be cognizant of the opportunity to scrutinize the authenticity of SNS evidence in the deposition portion of the proceedings or related proceedings.

Second, an inspection of computers and cell phones can provide information about the history of Internet use as well as an "evidentiary trail" that could be used to determine whether the subject hardware was the actual device used in the origination of the proposed SNS profile and posting. [*Id.* at 427-28.] Litigants should give careful consideration to the types and availability of devices, as well as the distinctive characteristics that associate a party with specific hardware, to ensure that the device and content are properly authenticated.

Third, a subpoena issued to SNS providers seeking information relating to users' accounts and profiles provides another critical source for litigants as a means of properly authenticating SNS content submitted as evidence. [*Id.* at 428.] [Please see Section III of Chapter 3 for detailed discussions of problems and challenges in seeking social media data directly from social media providers.]

> **PRACTICE POINTER**
>
> *Real Time Activity:* In cases where the person may be using her real name, but denies that she made a particular comment or post, Facebook gives posters the option of deleting their post or comment at any time, so the fact that the post was left for a period of time is further evidence that it was either authored or approved by the Facebook user. In the case of spam posts (unsolicited posts or messages that appear on a Facebook wall, for example, that are typically triggered by a virus or uninvited user), it is not uncommon for the person's Facebook friends to alert them to repeated, duplicate postings, and for the person to post something in apology for it. Again, the real time activity on social media provides insight into the authenticity of the post(s) being offered into evidence. Similarly, people with a Twitter account, for example, have the option of posting a follow up tweet in which they disavow a tweet as not being authored by them.
>
> *Educate Deponent on Risks of Providing False Testimony:* One potential tactic is to signal to the suspected author in deposition questioning that resistance would be futile. For example, before asking the suspected author to confirm the authenticity of the posting, you might ask questions, such as "Are you aware that the author's computer contains unique identifying information that allows someone to determine the source of a posting?" Such questioning will educate the witness on the risks of providing false testimony, making it more likely that the witness will authenticate the disputed information.

3. Admissibility of Potentially Relevant Evidence

[4:5] **Exclusions and Exceptions to the Hearsay Rule:** There are several reported cases in which evidence from social networking websites have been addressed. In general, courts are applying the rules of evidence and, in particular, exceptions to the hearsay rule to determine whether the evidence should be admitted.

In applying exceptions to the hearsay rule, courts seem to be treating posts from social media and the Internet as the same as statements from conversations or written documents.

[4:5:1] **Use of Information as Prior Inconsistent Statements:** Court held that the victim's statements on her Myspace profile were admissible as prior inconsistent statements to impeach her testimony and should have been admitted by the trial court [see, e.g., *In re K.W.*, 666 S.E.2d 490, 494 (N.C. Ct. App. 2008)]. In a termination of parental rights case, the court considered the father's statement on his Myspace profile that he did not want children. [*In re T.T.*, 228 S.W.3d 312, 322-23 (Tex. Ct. App. 2007).]

[4:5:2] **Use of Information as a Party Admission:** A common issue is whether a disputed posting by a non-party employee may be classified as the employer's party admission. Here, too, a company's social media policy and monitoring of social media activity may be relevant considerations. The proponent of the evidence may argue that an employee was acting within the course and scope of employment, either because the activity was somehow encouraged by the company's social media policy or because the activity was monitored by the company. Of course, this argument will be stronger in the following situations: if the employee was discussing a topic related to the company's business; if it could be shown that the company's customers frequented the same site or even read or responded to postings; or if other co-workers coordinated or discussed activity on the site internally.

Chapter Contents

Chapter 5: Use of Social Media During Trial

Chapter 5

Use of Social Media During Trial

1. Introduction

[5:1] **Social Media Is Becoming Critical to a Fair Trial:** The use of Facebook, Twitter, YouTube, and other social media has become an issue in the continuing effort to provide a fair trial. Use of the Internet has also become a major issue. There are a number of reasons that judges, lawyers, and jurors need to pay attention to the myriad uses of social media during trials. This chapter will look at these new challenges to the right to a fair trial.

2. Jury Summons, Questionnaires, and Instructions

[5:2] **Simpler and More Direct Language Regarding Use of Social Media in Jury Summons and Questionnaires:**

[5:2:1] **Jury Summons Should Specifically State that Jurors May Not Seek Out Any Information About the Case on Social Media Sites:** In *Russo v. Takata Corporation*, one of the jurors Googled the defendant and reviewed its website after receiving a jury summons. [774 N.W.2d 441 (S.D. 2009).] The juror failed to mention that research during *voir dire*. However, during deliberations, he reported his research to the other jurors. His research was material to an issue in dispute and contrary to the evidence in the record. After a defense verdict, Plaintiff moved for a new trial. In a footnote to the opinion awarding a new trial, the South Dakota Supreme Court mentioned that the jury summons stated "Do not seek out evidence regarding this case or the questionnaire with anyone." The Court acknowledged that the statement may not have put the juror on notice that performing a Google search on Defendant constituted seeking out evidence. The Court suggested that lower courts "consider using simpler and more direct language in the summons to indicate that no information about the case or the parties should be sought out by any means, including via computer searches."

[5:2:2] **Juror Questionnaires Should Specifically Instruct Jurors Not to Use Social Media to Obtain or Share Information About the Case:** Since January 1, 2010, a federal rule requires that all juror questionnaires contain a cover sheet with the following statement: "You may not do research about any issues involved in the case. You may not blog, Tweet, or use the Internet to obtain or share information." [http://tinyurl.com/9xvwjus]

[5:2:2:1] **The New York Committee on Criminal Jury Instructions Provides Excellent Suggested Language to Include in Juror Questionnaires:** The New York Committee on Criminal Jury Instructions revised its preliminary instructions to jurors on May 5, 2009. In *People v. Jamison*, the Court described the new instructions to include "specific instructions to jurors not to use 'Internet maps or Google Earth' as well as not to actually visit any place mentioned during the trial, not to use 'the Internet' to do any research about the case, and not to use 'text messages, e-mail, Internet chat or chat rooms, blogs, or social websites, such as Facebook, Myspace, or Twitter' as well as face-to-face conversations to discuss the case." [No. 8042/06, 2009 WL 2568740, at *6 (N.Y. Sup. Ct. Aug. 18, 2009).]

[5:2:2:2] **The Committee on Court Administration Has Similarly Provided Excellent Model Language to Include in Juror Questionnaires:** The Committee on Court Administration and Case Management of the Judicial Conference of the United States, a rule-making body for all federal courts, proposed a model jury instruction that states, *inter alia*, "I know that many of you use cell phones, Blackberries, the Internet and other tools of technology. You also must not talk to anyone about this case or use these tools to communicate electronically with anyone about the case . . . You may not communicate with anyone about the case on your cell phone, through e-mail, Blackberry, iPhone, text messaging, or on Twitter, through any blog or website, through any Internet chat room, or by way of any other social networking websites, including Facebook, Myspace, LinkedIn, or YouTube."

> **PRACTICE POINTER**
>
> Prior to trial, attorneys do well to review the juror questionnaire forms used in the court where the trial will be held. If they do not contain the above model language, attorneys should consider making a formal request that the court include the model language addressing the use of social media in its juror questionnaires and even juror summons.

3. The Use of Social Media to Conduct Research on Jurors

[5:3] **Discover Trends of Thought, Attitudes, and Opinions of the Jury Pool Prior to Trial Via Social Media:** In addition to researching individual jurors, parties should also consider social media research to discover trends of thought, attitudes, opinions, and the like among the jury pool in the area, particularly in a high profile case. Indeed, information obtained from social media sites may be different from that found in traditional media outlets and, most importantly, closer to the actual opinion of the potential jurors than the views expressed in traditional media. In-depth social media research includes not only user-generated content on traditional social media sites (including blogs), but also user comments on other sites such as traditional media sites. Notably, comprehensive social media research, typically conducted by experienced jury research consultants, can be useful not only in the planning phase of the case, but also for change of venue motions when a party may be trying to establish potential juror bias or the like.

[5:4] **Attorney Use of Social Media in the Courtroom:** Attorneys have another tool available to them in cases where the jurors are identified by their full name and not just a juror number. Although the case law is not well developed in this area, recent decisions suggest attorneys may research prospective jurors using social media *and* can do it in the courtroom during jury selection.

[5:4:1] **Attorneys May Conduct Internet Research During Jury Selection:** In *Carino v. Muenzen*, the New Jersey court issued a press release before trial in which the court stated that wireless Internet access was now available to "maximize productivity for attorneys" and other court users. [*Carino v.*

Muenzen, No. L-0028-7, 2010 WL 3448071 (N.J. Super. Ct. App. Div. Aug. 30, 2010)]. During the *voir dire*, the plaintiff's attorney in this medical malpractice case searched the Internet for information about potential jurors. Defense counsel objected, and the trial judge directed the plaintiff's attorney to close his laptop. The trial judge reasoned that Plaintiff's counsel had an unfair advantage during jury selection because Plaintiff's counsel had not told defense counsel before the trial that he intended to use his laptop to research potential jurors.

Plaintiff's counsel appealed, and while the appellate court did not reverse the trial court, it reasoned that Plaintiff's counsel did not have an unfair advantage during jury selection because the court had announced the availability of wireless Internet access in the courthouse before trial, and there was no state court rule requiring a lawyer to notify the court or an adversary about his use of the Internet at trial. (Ultimately, the court of appeal chose not to reverse the trial court because appellant had failed to demonstrate any prejudice resulting from the trial court's ruling.)

PRACTICE POINTER

Many courts provide WiFi and attorneys do well to consider accessing the Internet and social media sites to learn about prospective jurors during *voir dire*. Of course, it is best to have two to three attorneys conducting the *voir dire* analysis simultaneously otherwise it may be difficult to access the data, record it, and then use it in the form of specific questions.

4. Monitoring the Jury Through Social Media During Trial

[5:5] **Using Social Media to Reveal Jury Misconduct:** Using social media to get more information on your jury should not end with picking a jury, but should continue throughout the trial as Figure 5.1 illustrates:

[5:5:1] **Posting Comments Indicating Prejudice Against Defendant:** In one widely reported case, a criminal defense attorney's son found a troubling Facebook post while doing further research on the jurors in a resisting arrest case. In that case, Juror Hadley Jons did not wait until jury deliberations to make this post: "gonna be fun to tell the defendant they're GUILTY" [see Fig. 5.1].

Figure 5.1 A Juror's Facebook Post

[5:5:2] **Social Media Reveals Juror Not Truthful During Voir Dire:** In *State v. Dellinger*, Juror Amber Hyre sent a message to the defendant and appellant on Myspace. [*State v. Dellinger*, 696 S.E.2d 40 (W. Va. 2010).] After she sent this message, Juror Hyre and Dellinger became Myspace friends and could read postings on each other's pages. More significantly, when all the prospective jurors were asked if they had a business or social relationship with Dellinger, Juror Hyre did not say anything. Juror Hyre also failed to disclose that she was related by marriage to a witness, or her close friendship with the witness's daughter. During the trial, Juror Hyre posted on Myspace about being in court that day but did not post anything substantive about the case. The trial court did not fault her for any of her postings.

On appeal, Dellinger argued that Juror Hyre's lack of candor on *voir dire* should have been grounds for a new trial. The Court of Appeal reversed and ordered a new trial. The Court of Appeal held that "'there is a fine line between being willing to serve and being anxious . . . . The individual who lies in order to improve his chances of service has too much of a stake in the matter to be considered indifferent.'" [*Id.* at 44 (quoting *Dyer v. Calderon*, 151 F.3d 970, 982 (9th Cir. 1998), http://tinyurl.com/8kltebu] "In this case, we hold that the trial court was clearly wrong in finding Juror Hyre to be a 'fair and impartial juror.' To the contrary, as demonstrated by the facts set forth above, Juror Hyre intentionally and repeatedly failed to be forthcoming about her connections to Appellant and witnesses Frame and Slaughter, arguably, in order to improve her chances of serving on Appellant's jury." [*Id.* at 44.]

[5:5:3] **Monitoring Reveals Juror Blogging About the Case During Trial:** In a murder case in Ventura, California, a juror blogged about the case during the trial. In his blog called "The Misanthrope," the juror posted photographs of the murder weapon – a 15-inch, double-edged, saw-toothed knife. The juror also complained about the length of the 19-day trial, and was critical of the court's staff. He also had a chat room set up so that visitors to the blog could ask him questions about the trial. The defense attorneys learned of the blog, and informed the judge. Ventura County Superior Court Judge Edward Brodie cited the juror for contempt of court because he had not refrained from discussing the case. The defense also moved for a new trial during the sentencing phase based on juror misconduct. The court denied the motion, but it will be an issue on appeal when the defendant appeals his 27-year sentence.

> **PRACTICE POINTER**
>
> *Jury Instructions Should Specifically Address the Use of Social Media during the Trial:* Counsel for the parties should make a point of asking the court to instruct the jury not to discuss the case on Facebook, Twitter, LinkedIn, a blog, or any social media and to remind the jury at different times during the trial. Even vague references to the case should not be permitted. If the jury is specifically instructed not to discuss the case on social media, and ignores this instruction, then the facts may be stronger for the court granting a motion for new trial [see Appendix B for proposed Jury Instructions].
>
> *Use Social Media to Learn Important Details:* As the above cases demonstrate, research on social media during the entirety of the trial may result in important details about the fairness of the trial and may even reveal a blog site or posts that can support a request to the court that the prospective juror be excused for cause.

5. Real-Time Feeds and Live Blogging by People in the Courtroom (Other Than Jurors)

[5:6] **Circumvention of Sequestration Orders:** Another possible issue that counsel may encounter involves the role of social networking sites in the real-time reporting of trials from the courtroom, typically via live-feed websites like Twitter, by people in the courtroom other than jurors.

[5:6:1] **Tweets During Trial by Student Observers Read by Witnesses:** In *United States v. W.R. Grace*, the court permitted the University of Montana Law School and School of Journalism to cover the trial in real time. Each day, students published detailed accounts of the trial testimony via Twitter and chronicled the trial's events on a blog. Although witnesses had been sequestered, the government's key witness nevertheless read about the trial testimony online, a fact that he admitted during cross-examination. The defense accused the witness of fabricating testimony based on his review of the real-time accounts of two other witnesses. Indeed, the district court later struck the testimony of this witness against one of the defendants and issued a harsh jury instruction regarding his credibility. [see Order, *United States v. W.R. Grace*, 455 F. Supp. 2d 1199 (D. Mont. 2009), http://tinyurl.com/9hqjtyx; Jury Instruction, *United States v. W.R. Grace*, (D. Mont. 2009)].

PRACTICE POINTER

Counsel should be aware of any live blogging or tweeting from the courtroom. In making a request for witness sequestration, counsel should ask the court to prohibit witnesses from following online updates of the trial. During trial, the trial team must read any Twitter and real-time blog coverage of the case. This will assist counsel in determining whether a witness has based his testimony on online information concerning the testimony of another witness.

---

6. Use of Social Media During Trial May Lead to Mistrial

[5:7] **Decision on Mistrial Hinges on Whether Extrinsic Evidence Caused Prejudice:** When a juror inappropriately uses social media during trial, various remedies are possible, including a mistrial, but if the juror does not introduce extrinsic evidence into the jury deliberations, the misconduct may be remedied simply by dismissal of the juror or by a curative instruction. Even if the juror introduces extrinsic evidence into the deliberations, the conduct still must be sufficiently prejudicial to warrant a mistrial. Reviewing some results is instructive:

[5:7:1] **Juror's Credible Explanations for Posts, the Lack of Prejudice to Defendant, *and No Extrinsic Evidence*—No Mistrial:** In *United States v. Vincent J. Fumo*, the Eastern District addressed Twitter and Facebook posts juror Eric Wuest made during jury deliberations. [*United States v. Vincent J. Fumo*, No. 06-319, 2009 U.S. Dist. LEXIS 51581 (E.D. Pa. June 17, 2009).] Wuest was a juror on the corruption trial of Vincent Fumo. Among his posts, Wuest tweeted "This is it . . . no looking back now!" On March 13, 2009, he posted the following comment to his Facebook page: "Stay tuned for the big announcement on Monday everyone." After the jury had reached its verdict but before the verdict was announced, a news report revealed such posts. The Court called Wuest in and examined Wuest at length about the postings. Satisfied with Wuest's explanations, the Court allowed him to remain on the jury. Ultimately, Fumo was convicted on 137 of 139 charges. Fumo moved for a mistrial based on Wuest's conduct. In the June 17, 2009, opinion, the Court examined each of Wuest's posts. Finding that Wuest violated the Court's jury instructions not to discuss the case outside the courtroom by making the posts, the Court nevertheless found that Wuest's misconduct was harmless. Specifically, the Court found there was no evidence that Wuest was influenced by third-parties and no evidence that Wuest discussed his postings with the other jurors. In light of Wuest's credible explanations and the lack of prejudice, the Court denied the motion.

[5:7:2] **Juror Access of On-Line Data and Introduction of This Extrinsic Evidence into Jury Deliberations I—New Trial:** In *Russo*, the South Dakota Supreme Court granted a mistrial, allowing Plaintiff to retry a personal injury case which had resulted in a defense verdict. At issue was whether Defendant had notice of an alleged defect in the seat belt assembly it manufactured. At trial, Plaintiff introduced evidence establishing that other lawsuits had been filed against Defendant regarding the failure of the seat belt. After receiving his summons, a juror Googled the defendant and viewed its website. During jury deliberations, he disclosed his research and reported that the website did not identify any prior lawsuits. The South Dakota Supreme Court found that by making such disclosure the juror impermissibly introduced extrinsic evidence prejudicial to Plaintiff's case and awarded a new trial.

[5:7:3] **Juror Access of On-Line Data and Introduction of This Extrinsic Evidence into Jury Deliberations II — New Trial:** In *Wardlaw* v. *Maryland*, the Maryland Court of Special Appeals granted a mistrial in a sexual assault case. [971 A.3d 331 (Md. App. 2009).] In this case, testimony from a specialist indicated that the victim had ODD. A juror researched ODD on the Internet and determined that lying was associated with the condition. She reported her findings to her fellow jurors, who promptly reported her conduct to the Court. Even though this extrinsic evidence may have actually aided the defendant by casting doubt on the veracity of victim's story, the Court found upon the defendant's motion that the juror engaged in egregious misconduct requiring a new trial.

[5:7:4] **Juror Access of On-Line Data and Introduction of This Extrinsic Evidence into Jury Deliberations III — New Trial:** In *United States* v. *Bristol-Martir*, the First Circuit granted a mistrial. [971 A.3d 331 (Md. App. 2009).] The case involved charges of conspiracy to distribute narcotics against several police officers. During deliberations, one juror used the Internet to research the definitions of distribution and possession. Although the District Court dismissed the juror and issued curative instructions, the First Circuit found that a mistrial was necessary because the steps taken by the District Court could not cure the prejudice.

PRACTICE POINTER

These cases demonstrate that to avoid the waste and expense of a mistrial, both parties have an interest in ensuring that jurors do not access and use extrinsic evidence from social media sources in their deliberations. For this reason, counsel would do well to use clear and direct jury instructions that admonish jurors against such access and use.

Appendix A

Sample Interrogatories

SAMPLE INTERROGATORY NO. 1: State the name, web address, and user name for all blogs, online forums, and social networking websites that [Plaintiff/Defendant] has belonged or had membership to from [_____] to the present.

SAMPLE INTERROGATORY NO. 2: Identify the user name and e-mail address for any Facebook account maintained by YOU from [_____] through the present.

SAMPLE INTERROGATORY NO. 3: Identify the user name, registration information, account detail, login information, and any other identifying information for any job board or job search websites for which YOU are (or were) registered or of which YOU are (or were) a member, including but not limited to: Hot Jobs, Career Builder, Monster, job.com and salesjobhunter.com from [_____] through the present.

Sample Document Requests

SAMPLE REQUEST NO. 1: All online, profiles, comments, post-ings, messages (including without limitation, tweets, replies, retweets, direct messages, status updates, wall comments, groups joined, activity streams and blog entries), photographs, videos, e-mails, and online communications (including those posted by [Plaintiff/Defendant] or anyone on [Plaintiff's/Defendant's] behalf on social networking website), from [_____] to the present that:

1. refer or relate to the allegations set forth in the complaint;

2. refer or relate to any facts or defenses raised in the answer.

SAMPLE REQUEST NO. 2: For each social networking website account maintained by YOU, please produce YOUR account data for the period [_____] through the present. YOU may download and print YOUR social networking website data by logging onto YOUR Facebook account, selecting "Account Set-tings" under the "Account" tab on YOUR homepage, clicking on the "Learn More" link beside the "Download Your Informa-tion" tab, and following the directions on the "Download Your Information" page.

SAMPLE REQUEST NO. 3: All photographs or videos posted by [_____] or anyone on his or her behalf on social networking website(s) from [_____] to the present [see *Equal Employment Opportunity Commission v. Simply Storage Management, LLC*, 270 F.R.D. 430, 432 (S.D. Ind. 2010)].

SAMPLE REQUEST NO. 4: Electronic copies of [_____]'s com-plete profile on social networking website(s) (including all updates, changes, or modifications on [_____]'s profile) and all status updates, messages, wall comments, causes joined, groups joined, activity streams, blog entries, details, blurbs, comments, and applications for the period from [_____] to the present. To the extent electronic copies are not available, please provide the documents in hard copy form [see *Equal Employment Opportunity Commission v. Simply Storage Management, LLC,* 270 F.R.D. 430, 432 (S.D. Ind. 2010)].

Sample Deposition Questions

Does your company have a social media site, which company employees can use to post or exchange information?

- What is the name of the site?

- If we wanted to see the information placed on the company social media site, what would be the best way to see it?

- Are there private postings or communications that are private or only viewable by employees?

  - Do I have your permission, without a court order, to see what you have posted there?

Do you have any social media account where you post personal information about yourself?

- Which ones do you use?

  - Have you had other social media accounts that you no longer use?

- What name(s) do you use for yourself for your social media account(s)?

- If we wanted to see the information you post on your social media account(s), what would be the best way to see it?

- Do I have your permission, without a court order, to see what you have posted on your social media account(s)?

Have you ever posted comments in any Internet blog?

- Was it a personal blog, company blog, or something else?
- What was the name(s) of the blog(s)?
- What was the subject matter?
- When did you do the blogging?
- What name(s) did you use?
- If we wanted to see the information you put on this blog what would be the best way to find it?

Appendix B

Proposed Jury Instructions

Courts have responded appropriately and have included social media in the jury instructions before the trial begins and also prior to the beginning of the jury's deliberations.

At the Beginning of the Trial:

You, as jurors, must decide this case based solely on the evidence presented here within the four walls of this courtroom. This means that during the trial you must not conduct any independent research about this case, the matters in the case, or the individuals or corporations involved in the case. In other words, you should not consult dictionaries or reference materials; search the Internet, websites, or blogs; or use any other electronic tools to obtain information about this case or to help you decide the case. Please do not try to find out information from any source outside the confines of this courtroom.

Until you retire to deliberate, you may not discuss this case with anyone, not even your fellow jurors. After you retire to deliberate, you may begin discussing the case with your fellow jurors, but you cannot discuss the case with anyone else until you have returned a verdict and the case is at an end.

I know that many of you use cell phones, Blackberries, the Internet, and other tools of technology. You also must not talk to anyone at any time about this case or use these tools to communicate electronically with anyone about the case. This includes your family and friends. You may not communicate with anyone about the case on your cell phone, through e-mail, Blackberry, iPhone, or text messaging; or on Twitter, or through any blog or website, including Facebook, Google+, Myspace, LinkedIn, or YouTube. You may not use any similar technology of social media, even if I have not specifically mentioned it here. I expect you will inform me as soon as you become aware of another juror's violation of these instructions.

At the Close of the Case:

During your deliberations, you must not communicate with or provide any information to anyone by any means about this case. You may not use any electronic device or media, such as a telephone, a cell phone, a smart phone, an iPhone, or a Blackberry; or computer, the Internet, any Internet service, or any text or instant messaging service; or any Internet chat room, blog, or website, such as Facebook, Myspace, LinkedIn, YouTube or Twitter, to communicate to anyone any information about this case or to conduct any research about this case until I accept your verdict. In other words, you cannot talk to anyone on the phone, correspond with anyone, or electronically communicate with anyone about this case.

You can only discuss the case in the jury room with your fellow jurors during deliberations. I expect you will inform me as soon as you become aware of another juror's violation of these instructions.

You may not use these electronic means to investigate or communicate about the case because it is important that you decide this case based solely on the evidence presented in this courtroom. Information on the Internet or available through social media might be wrong, incomplete, or inaccurate. You are only permitted to discuss the case with your fellow jurors during deliberations because they have seen and heard the same evidence you have. In our judicial system, it is important that you are not influenced by anything or anyone outside of this courtroom. Otherwise, your decision may be based on information known only by you and not your fellow jurors or the parties in the case. This would unfairly and adversely affect the judicial process.

http://www.uscourts.gov/uscourts/News/2012/jury-instructions.pdf

Appendix C

Third-Party Social Media Provider Preservation Notice

[DATE]

[NAME]

[ADDRESS]

Re: **DOCUMENT PRESERVATION NOTICE**

Dear [NAME]:

I am writing to notify you that my client, [NAME], is engaged in a lawsuit with [OPPOSING PARTY] regarding [DESCRIPTION OF SUIT'S SUBJECT MATTER]. Consequently, [CLIENT'S NAME] is required to preserve all evidence potentially relevant to this suit, including evidence in the possession, custody, or control of third-party social media websites like [NAME OF THIRD-PARTY SOCIAL MEDIA PROVIDER].

Following an internal investigation, [CLIENT'S NAME], has determined that the [FACEBOOK, MYSPACE, TWITTER, ETC.] accounts of the following individuals may contain information relevant to this suit:

[NAMES OF SOCIAL   [CORRESPONDING URL TO
MEDIA USERS]   SOCIAL USER'S MEDIA PAGE]

_____   _____

_____   _____

_____   _____

_____   _____

_____   _____

We thus request that you immediately take all necessary steps to ensure the preservation of all documents and electronically stored information, including metadata associated with the above users and their accounts.

I will be in touch shortly to discuss how best to retrieve the information we seek to preserve. In the meantime, please do not hesitate to contact me at [PHONE NUMBER]. Thank you for your cooperation.

Sincerely,

[COUNSEL'S NAME]

Appendix D

Litigation Hold Memorandum to Client

To: [KEY PLAYERS; IT DEPARTMENT; RECORDS MANAGE-
MENT DEPARTMENT]

From: [GENERAL COUNSEL; PRESIDENT; CEO]

Cc: [OUTSIDE COUNSEL]

Re: **Document Preservation Obligations Regarding**
[ABBREVIATED NAME OF LITIGATION]

DO NOT FORWARD

ATTORNEY-CLIENT PRIVILEGED AND CONFIDENTIAL COMMUNICATION

On [DATE] this company was named as a defendant in [NAME OF LITIGATION]. As part of the litigation process, [CLIENT] ("the Company") is required by law to preserve all documents and records relevant to the litigation. You have been identified as a person who may have relevant documents and data, and the Legal Department requires your assistance to preserve all corporate information related to the litigation. [MODIFY IF COMPANY *ANTICIPATES* LITIGATION]

The directive in this memorandum is extremely important; please read it carefully and do not forward it without permission of the sender. Please note that the instructions contained in this memorandum supersede any other record retention policy. Potentially relevant documents must therefore be preserved even if the Company's record-keeping guidelines would normally allow you to delete or destroy material.

1. Severe Consequences for Failure to Comply with This Directive

The failure to preserve relevant documents and data can result in severe sanctions against the Company. Thus, it is of critical importance that you comply with the instructions below. Please note that you may be called to give testimony about your document- and data-preservation efforts.

2. The Matter

[DESCRIBE THE RELEVANT SUBJECT MATTER OF THE LITIGATION OR POTENTIAL LITIGATION. NOTE THAT IN THIS SECTION YOU SHOULD NOT DISCUSS LITIGATION STRATEGY BECAUSE YOU MAY NEED TO PRODUCE THIS DOCUMENT AT A LATER DATE.]

3. General Instructions

Your only obligation at this time is to identify and preserve relevant documents. Please do not sort, categorize, index, or summarize any documents—including electronic documents—that are responsive to this memorandum. Rather, only identify them and preserve them intact in the way that they were collected or created and filed in the ordinary course of business (e.g., if you created a personal folder in your e-mail, leave it intact and do not try to copy it to a CD or external drive).

4. The Types of Documents and Data That You Must Retain

You must maintain both hard copies of documents as well as all e-mail and other electronically stored information. Please note that you are required to preserve all non-identical copies of potentially relevant documents. If one copy contains handwritten notes and the other does not, for example, you must preserve both copies. Drafts of potentially relevant documents should also be preserved.

The term "documents" includes handwritten notes, drafts, tabulations, calculations, summaries, and work papers; it is not limited only to "formal" or "final" documents. Examples of documents (whether in electronic or hard copy) that should be retained include [MODIFY AS APPROPRIATE]:

- Letters,
- Correspondence,
- Memoranda,
- Reports,
- Invoices,
- External and internal literature,
- Schedules,
- Worksheets,
- Plans,
- Minutes,
- Bulletins,
- Brochures,
- Catalogs,
- Notices,

- Press releases,
- Transcripts.
- Calendars,
- Diaries,
- Charts, and
- Forecasts.

This list is not exhaustive; it is provided by way of example only, and all documents relating in any way to the topics discussed in this memorandum must be preserved. If you are unsure about the relevance of a document, be cautious and preserve it.

Examples of electronic information that you may need to retain includes, but are not limited to [MODIFY AS APPROPRIATE]:

E-mail messages and their attachments, including messages in your Inbox, Sent Items, and Deleted Items folders, in any personal folders and in any other e-mail accounts you may use, including personal accounts;

Information, including but not limited to pictures, messages, and postings on [CLIENT]'s or your personal social media websites or web pages (e.g., Facebook, Myspace, Twitter, LinkedIn, etc.);

- Other Internet website or blog posts;
- Internet history and activity logs;
- Word-processing documents;
- Electronic spreadsheets;
- Electronic calendars;
- Electronic versions of documents, such as contracts, drafts of contracts, internal and external memoranda, and board meeting minutes and agendas;
- Taped or recorded messages, calls, or meetings;
- Instant messages or other chat messages and/or message history.

To comply with this memorandum, you may be required to preserve electronic information found in the following sources:

- Internet pages,
- Internet records,
- Networks,
- Computer systems (including legacy systems no longer used by the Company in its normal course of business),
- Servers,
- Archives,
- Backup and disaster-recovery systems,
- Tapes,
- Disks,
- Drives,
- Cartridges,
- Computers, including laptops and personal home computers,
- Portable hard drives,
- Memory cards,
- "Thumb drives,"
- Personal digital assistants, and
- Mobile telephones and smartphones.

AS YOU CONDUCT YOUR SEARCH FOR POTENTIALLY RELEVANT INFORMATION PLEASE REMEMBER THAT YOU MUST MAKE DILIGENT AND REASONABLE EFFORTS TO PRESERVE RESPONSIVE DOCUMENTS IN ALL LOCATIONS WHERE THEY MAY BE FOUND.

5. The Categories of Documents and Data You Must Retain

Documents you must retain include those that *mention, discuss, or relate* to any of the following subjects:

[INSERT CATEGORIES OF RELEVANT AND POTENTIALLY RELE-VANT TOPICS PERTAINING TO THE LITIGATION/ANTICIPATED LITIGATION]

There may be other categories of documents relevant to these issues. If you are unsure about the relevance of a document, **be cautious and preserve it**.

Do not discard any documents (including all forms of electronic messages, including e-mails and messages on social media websites) relating to these topics or any other aspect of the [NAME OF LITIGATION] litigation. This request applies to documents now in your possession, as well as those you create or receive subsequent to this memorandum. We also ask that you not create any documents in response to this memorandum.

Normal attorney-client privilege will apply to many documents. Thus, as with all attorney-client consultations, you should be assured that the document itself may remain confidential. You must, however, take the ordinary steps to preserve the attorney-client privilege (i.e., not sharing the document with non-lawyers unless they have a need to know and not sharing the document with those outside the Company).

6. Suspension of Document-Destruction Policies

Please suspend all standard document-destruction programs, including programs or processes that automatically delete electronic information at the conclusion of a set period of time. Destruction of backup tapes must be suspended, as well as any process that overwrites or destroys potentially relevant information. If you are unsure whether some of your electronic information is subject to routine destruction, please contact [NAME] in the IT Department at [TELEPHONE NUMBER].

7. Please Err on the Side of Retaining Documents and Contact [NAME OF LEGAL CONTACT] with Any Questions Regarding This Memorandum or Document Preservation

We understand that these categories of information are broad; however, we do not know at this time which specific documents or categories of documents may be requested. As a result, the Company must ensure that **all** documents of potential relevance are preserved. If you are not sure whether particular documents or records should be retained, please err on the side of caution; you must not destroy, discard, or delete those documents without prior approval from [NAME OF LEGAL CONTACT]. If you have questions as to whether particular documents should be preserved, please contact [NAME OF LEGAL CONTACT]. **Further, if you believe that an employee who has documents or records subject to this directive has not been advised of his or her preservation obligations, please contact [NAME OF LEGAL CONTACT] with the name of that employee.**

8. Confidentiality

Please do not discuss the lawsuit or any potential claims or issues with anyone outside the Company unless specifically directed otherwise. This letter is confidential and its contents may not be shared or discussed. Do not forward or distribute this memorandum without the permission of the sender.

Acknowledgment

I have reviewed the above memorandum and agree to follow the preservation instructions therein.

Name (printed): _____

Signature: _____

Date: _____

IMAGE CREDITS

Figure 1.1   Social Networking Growth Chart, May 2010. http://www.pewinternet.org. Used by permission of Pew Research Center

Figure 3.1   Will Ferrell Tweet, May 2010. http://www.stevenhumour.com. Courtesy of Steven Humour Blog.

Figure 3.2   Facebook Privacy Page Screenshot, July 2012. Used by permission of Facebook

Figure 3.3   Judge Kozinski Article Screenshot, July 2009. Courtesy of Bill Mears and CNN.com

Index

A

B

C

D

K

J

L

SELECTED BOOKS FROM

The Lawyer's Guide to Microsoft Word 2010
By Ben M. Schorr

Product Code: 5110721 / LPM Price: $41.95 / Regular Price: $69.95

Microsoft® Word is one of the most used applications in the Microsoft® Office suite. This handy reference includes clear explanations, legal-specific descriptions, and time-saving tips for getting the most out of Microsoft Word—and customizing it for the needs of today's legal professional. Focusing on the tools and features that are essential for lawyers in their everyday practice, this book explains in detail the key components to help make you more effective, more efficient, and more successful.

Google for Lawyers: Essential Search Tips and Productivity Tools
By Carole A. Levitt and Mark E. Rosch

Product Code: 5110704 / LPM Price: $47.95 / Regular Price: $79.95

This book introduces novice Internet searchers to the diverse collection of information locatable through Google. The book discusses the importance of including effective Google searching as part of a lawyer's due diligence, and cites case law that mandates that lawyers should use Google and other resources available on the Internet, where applicable. For intermediate and advanced users, the book unlocks the power of various advanced search strategies and hidden search features they might not be aware of.

Blogging in One Hour for Lawyers
By Ernie Svenson

Product Code: 5110744 / LPM Price: $24.95 / Regular Price: $39.95

Until a few years ago, only the largest firms could afford to engage an audience of millions. Now, lawyers in any size firm can reach a global audience at little to no cost—all because of blogs. An effective blog can help you promote your practice, become more "findable" online, and take charge of how you are perceived by clients, journalists and anyone who uses the Internet. Blogging in One Hour for Lawyers will show you how to create, maintain, and improve a legal blog—and gain new business opportunities along the way. In just one hour, you will learn to:

- Set up a blog quickly and easily
- Write blog posts that will attract clients
- Choose from various hosting options like Blogger, TypePad, and WordPress
- Make your blog friendly to search engines, increasing your ranking
- Tweak the design of your blog by adding customized banners and colors
- Easily send notice of your blog posts to Facebook and Twitter
- Monitor your blog's traffic with Google Analytics and other tools
- Avoid ethics problems that may result from having a legal blog

The Electronic Evidence and Discovery Handbook: Forms, Checklists, and Guidelines
By Sharon D. Nelson, Bruce A. Olson, and John W. Simek

Product Code: 5110569 / LPM Price: $99.95 / Regular Price: $129.95

The use of electronic evidence has increased dramatically over the past few years, but many lawyers still struggle with the complexities of electronic discovery. This substantial book provides lawyers with the templates they need to frame their discovery requests and provides helpful advice on what they can subpoena. In addition to the ready-made forms, the authors also supply explanations to bring you up to speed on the electronic discovery field. The accompanying CD-ROM features over 70 forms, including, Motions for Protective Orders, Preservation and Spoliation Documents, Motions to Compel, Electronic Evidence Protocol Agreements, Requests for Production, Internet Services Agreements, and more. Also included is a full electronic evidence case digest with over 300 cases detailed!

Facebook in One Hour for Lawyers
By Dennis Kennedy and Allison C. Shields

Product Code: 5110745 / LPM Price: $24.95 / Regular Price: $39.95

With a few simple steps, lawyers can use Facebook® to market their services, grow their practices, and expand their legal network—all by using the same methods they already use to communicate with friends and family. Facebook® in One Hour for Lawyers will show any attorney—from Facebook® novices to advanced users—how to use this powerful tool for both professional and personal purposes.

LinkedIn in One Hour for Lawyers
By Dennis Kennedy and Allison C. Shields

Product Code: 5110737 / LPM Price: $19.95 / Regular Price: $34.95

Lawyers work in a world of networks, connections, referrals, and recommendations. For many lawyers, the success of these networks determines the success of their practice. LinkedIn®, the premier social networking tool for business, can help you create, nurture, and expand your professional network and gain clients in the process. LinkedIn® in One Hour for Lawyers provides an introduction to this powerful tool in terms that any attorney can understand. In just one hour, you will learn to:

- Set up a LinkedIn account
- Complete your basic profile
- Create a robust, dynamic profile that will attract clients
- Build your connections
- Use search tools to enhance your network
- Maximize your presence with features such as groups, updates, answers, and recommendations
- Monitor your network with ease
- Optimize your settings for privacy concerns
- Use LinkedIn® effectively in the hiring process
- Develop a LinkedIn strategy to grow your legal network

SELECTED BOOKS FROM

ABA LawPracticeManagementSection
MARKETING • MANAGEMENT • TECHNOLOGY • FINANCE

Virtual Law Practice: How to Deliver Legal Services Online
By Stephanie L. Kimbro

Product Code: 5110707 / LPM Price: $47.95 / Regular Price: $79.95

The legal market has recently experienced a dramatic shift as lawyers seek out alternative methods of practicing law and providing more affordable legal services. Virtual law practice is revolutionizing the way the public receives legal services and how legal professionals work with clients. If you are interested in this form of practicing law, *Virtual Law Practice* will help you:

- *Responsibly deliver legal services online to* your clients
- Successfully set up and operate a virtual law office
- Establish a virtual law practice online through a secure, client-specific portal
- Manage and market your virtual law practice
- Understand state ethics and advisory opinions
- Find more flexibility and work/life balance in the legal profession

Social Media for Lawyers: The Next Frontier
By Carolyn Elefant and Nicole Black

Product Code: 5110710 / LPM Price: $47.95 / Regular Price: $79.95

The world of legal marketing has changed with the rise of social media sites such as Linkedin, Twitter, and Facebook. Law firms are seeking their companies attention with tweets, videos, blog posts, pictures, and online content. Social media is fast and delivers news at record pace. This book provides you with a practical, goal-centric approach to using social media in your law practice that will enable you to identify social media platforms and tools that fit your practice and implement them easily, efficiently, and ethically.

iPad Apps in One Hour for Lawyers
By Tom Mighell

Product Code: 5110739 / LPM Price: $19.95 / Regular Price: $34.95

At last count, there were more than 80,000 apps available for the iPad. Finding the best apps often can be an overwhelming, confusing, and frustrating process. iPad Apps in One Hour for Lawyers provides the "best of the best" apps that are essential for any law practice. In just one hour, you will learn about the apps most worthy of your time and attention. This book will describe how to buy, install, and update iPad apps, and help you:

- Find apps to get organized and improve your productivity
- Create, manage, and store documents on your iPad
- Choose the best apps for your law office, including litigation and billing apps
- Find the best news, reading, and reference apps
- Take your iPad on the road with apps for travelers
- Maximize your social networking power
- Have some fun with game and entertainment apps during your relaxation time

Twitter in One Hour for Lawyers
By Jared Correia

Product Code: 5110746 / LPM Price: $24.95 / Regular Price: $39.95

More lawyers than ever before are using Twitter to network with colleagues, attract clients, market their law firms, and even read the news. But to the uninitiated, Twitter's short messages, or tweets, can seem like they are written in a foreign language. Twitter in One Hour for Lawyers will demystify one of the most important social-media platforms of our time and teach you to tweet like an expert. In just one hour, you will learn to:

- Create a Twitter account and set up your profile
- Read tweets and understand Twitter jargon
- Write tweets—and send them at the appropriate time
- Gain an audience—follow and be followed
- Engage with other Twitters users
- Integrate Twitter into your firm's marketing plan
- Cross-post your tweets with other social media platforms like Facebook and LinkedIn
- Understand the relevant ethics, privacy, and security concerns
- Get the greatest possible return on your Twitter investment
- And much more!

The Lawyer's Essential Guide to Writing
By Marie Buckley

Product Code: 5110726 / LPM Price: $47.95 / Regular Price: $79.95

This is a readable, concrete guide to contemporary legal writing. Based on Marie Buckley's years of experience coaching lawyers, this book provides a systematic approach to all forms of written communication, from memoranda and briefs to e-mail and blogs. The book sets forth three principles for powerful writing and shows how to apply those principles to develop a clean and confident style.

iPad in One Hour for Lawyers, Second Edition
By Tom Mighell

Product Code: 5110747 / LPM Price: $24.95 / Regular Price: $39.95

Whether you are a new or a more advanced iPad user, *iPad in One Hour for Lawyers* takes a great deal of the mystery and confusion out of using your iPad. Ideal for lawyers who want to get up to speed swiftly, this book presents the essentials so you don't get bogged down in technical jargon and extraneous features and apps. In just six, short lessons, you'll learn how to:

- Quickly Navigate and Use the iPad User Interface
- Set Up Mail, Calendar, and Contacts
- Create and Use Folders to Multitask and Manage Apps
- Add Files to Your iPad, and Sync Them
- View and Manage Pleadings, Case Law, Contracts, and other Legal Documents
- Use Your iPad to Take Notes and Create Documents
- Use Legal-Specific Apps at Trial or in Doing Research

30-DAY RISK-FREE ORDER FORM

ABA Law Practice Management Section
MARKETING • MANAGEMENT • TECHNOLOGY • FINANCE

Please print or type. To ship UPS, we must have your street address.
If you list a P.O. Box, we will ship by U.S. Mail.

Name

Member ID

Firm/Organization

Street Address

City/State/Zip

Area Code/Phone (In case we have a question about your order)

E-mail

Method of Payment:
❑ Check enclosed, payable to American Bar Association
❑ MasterCard   ❑ Visa   ❑ American Express

Card Number   Expiration Date

Signature Required

MAIL THIS FORM TO:
American Bar Association,
Publication Orders
P.O. Box 10892, Chicago, IL 60610

ORDER BY PHONE:
24 hours a day, 7 days a week:
Call 1-800-285-2221 to place a credit
card order. We accept Visa, MasterCard,
and American Express.

EMAIL ORDERS:
orders@americanbar.org
FAX: 1-312-988-5568

VISIT OUR WEB SITE:
www.ShopABA.org
Allow 7-10 days for regular UPS delivery.
Need it sooner? Ask about our overnight
delivery options. Call the ABA Service
Center at 1-800-285-2221 for more
information.

GUARANTEE:
If–for any reason–you are not satisfied
with your purchase, you may return it
within 30 days of receipt for a refund of
the price of the book(s).
No questions asked.

Thank You For Your Order.

Join the ABA Law Practice Management Section today and receive a substantial discount on Section publications!

Product Code:	Description:	Quantity:	Price:	Total Price:
				$
				$
				$
				$
				$

Shipping/Handling:		***Tax:**	Subtotal:	$
$0.00 to $9.99	add $0.00	IL residents add 9.75% DC residents add 6%	***Tax:**	$
$10.00 to $49.99	add $5.95			
$50.00 to $99.99	add $7.95		****Shipping/Handling:**	$
$100.00 to $199.99	add $9.95	Yes, I am an ABA member and would like to join the Law Practice Management Section today! (Add $50.00)		$
$200.00 to $499.99	add $12.95		**Total:**	$